PSYCHOTHERAPY AND SPIRITUAL DIRECTION

Other titles in the UKCP Series:

PSYCHOTHERAPY AND SPIRITUAL DIRECTION
Two Languages, One Voice?

Lynette Harborne

On behalf of the United Kingdom Council
for Psychotherapy

KARNAC

The author and publisher are grateful to the following for permission to quote the following material:

Madsen Gubi, P. (2010). *A qualitative exploration of the similarities and differences between Counselling and Spiritual Accompaniment* (pp. 8, 45, 54). Unpublished dissertation, Anglia Ruskin University.

First published in 2012 by
Karnac Books Ltd
118 Finchley Road
London NW3 5HT

British Library Cataloguing in Publication Data

A C.I.P. for this book is available from the British Library

ISBN-13: 978-1-78049-018-2

Typeset by V Publishing Solutions Pvt Ltd., Chennai, India

Printed in Great Britain

www.karnacbooks.com

This book is dedicated to my husband, Marcus, who has shared my journey most generously, even when the road has seemed full of potholes.

CONTENTS

ACKNOWLEDGEMENTS

Thanks are due to family, friends, and colleagues, who have shown endless patience in the face of my passion for my subject.

Thanks are due to clients, spiritual directees, supervisees, and supervisors, from whom I have learnt so much.

Thanks are due to my therapist and, over the years, to three spiritual directors, who have all been influential in my personal and spiritual formation as a therapist, as a spiritual director, and as a human being.

Thanks are due to that company of saints, in this world and the next, who have offered me love, support, and prayer during the difficult times.

ABOUT THE AUTHOR

Lynette Harborne is a UKCP registered psychotherapist and a BACP senior accredited therapist and supervisor. She works in private practice as a psychotherapist, supervisor, spiritual director, and trainer and is involved in the formation of seminarians and ordinands. She has an MSc in Integrative Psychotherapy and an MEd in Post-Compulsory Education. She has tutored counselling to Diploma Level and regularly examines MSc Psychotherapy students in viva examinations. She also has qualifications in supervision and coaching. She is currently Chair of the Association for Pastoral and Spiritual Care and Counselling (APSCC), a Division of BACP, and has recently chaired a research group investigating the inclusion of spirituality in BACP accredited training programmes. She has taken part in an APSCC research project investigating similarities and differences between psychotherapy and spiritual direction and edited the final report. She is also a member of the Planning Group of the Continuing the Journey Conference. She is the author of a number of papers.

PREFACE

My experience as a psychotherapist and spiritual director has raised my awareness that therapists are often uncomfortable when addressing overtly spiritual issues and that spiritual directors often lack confidence—and indeed competence—when faced with psychological questions. It is a desire to support practitioners in both areas in improving the service they offer their clients that has prompted me to write this book. As well as my interest in the healing benefits of the psychological process, I see the client's personal spirituality as a potentially potent resource to be harnessed in a genuinely holistic therapeutic enterprise.

In June 2008 I was invited to facilitate a day for spiritual directors on differences and similarities between spiritual direction and psychotherapy. One of the activities involved a Venn diagram with one set for therapy, one for direction, and the intersection for common factors. Initially the three sectors of the diagram were about the same size but, as my preparations for the day progressed, I found myself increasing the intersection until quite clearly it became the biggest sector, indicating that similarities far outweighed differences.

Since then my thinking has moved on much further and this book has grown out of my perhaps controversial belief that, essentially, psychotherapists and spiritual directors are offering the same thing. They both believe in the value of the individual and both commit themselves to a relationship with their clients through which personal growth and increased well-being may develop. True, there may be differences in terms of contract and content, but my experience of both over a number of years is that the process replicates that found in different models of therapy. Once I had come to this conclusion, the implications for both psychotherapists and spiritual directors became increasingly apparent and my exploration of these implications has resulted in this book.

While I realise that not everyone will accept my somewhat radical views, I nevertheless hope that the reader will be willing to share my interest and reflect on my proposition with an open mind.

FOREWORD

This is a book about the relationship between psychotherapy/counselling and spiritual direction/accompaniment. Both "professions" (or helping "ministries") originated as a ministry to the "soul", although psychotherapy moved away from its spiritual antecedents in its development of a quasi-scientific psychological understanding of the psyche that no longer included the spiritual. Yet recent developments in psychotherapy have begun to embrace what it means to work with human beings for whom spirituality is a significant aspect of their being, and to explore with them the ways in which they make meaning of life. Alongside these developments in psychotherapy, spiritual direction/accompaniment has developed both inside and outside the closet of the Church, and begun to recognise the need for a greater professionalism which creates the levels of trust and safety that enable more effective accompaniment and growth. Many of the spiritual insights gained by the forefathers of spiritual direction can be viewed as akin to many psychological insights, albeit they are often expressed in a different language of discourse. More psychotherapists are training in spiritual direction/accompaniment and vice versa, and, like Lynette Harborne, are seeing enough significant similarities to be exploring the possibility that they are, in fact, the same, and asking if they have anything to learn from each other.

In this book, Lynette Harborne, takes the reader through the developments in both ministries and sets the context in which she then generously enables us to share in her wisdom as an experienced and highly qualified psychotherapist and spiritual director. Her argument is informed by relevant literature and grounded in her personal experience and many discussions with others that have arisen in various training environments. Her forthright style of writing is thought-provoking. She leads the reader into a deeply considered and well-argued exposition which will challenge many practitioners in the disciplines of both psychotherapy and spiritual direction/accompaniment. Other psychotherapists and spiritual directors/accompaniers will breathe a sigh of relief that at last someone has spoken to their experiencing, has stopped accentuating the differences (if indeed there are any), and has made a convincing argument for raising the standard of competence in both. Lynette Harborne's book strengthens the case for greater professionalism and training in spiritual direction/accompaniment, and for greater openness to the spiritual in psychotherapy. It is clear that she values both "ministries" as a means of helping, and values the distinctive contribution of each to the development and welfare of others. She writes credibly on what she regards as being aspects that both ministries can learn from each other, including the need for training that includes an understanding of psychological process and the value of supervision in spiritual direction/accompaniment.

In her final Chapter, Lynette Harborne is deliberately and refreshingly provocative in asking what she calls "her heretical question"— "*Can spiritual direction be considered a modality of psychotherapy?*" Many practitioners may consider this to be a step too far, but if they can at least approach the argument that Lynette Harborne makes, with openness and humility, it will have significantly positive implications for both ministries and improve the levels of competence that each offers. That can only ever be beneficial for the people that we are trying to help.

Dr Peter Madsen Gubi
Senior Lecturer in Counselling, University of Central Lancashire
Spiritual Director & BACP Senior Accredited Counsellor & Supervisor in
Private Practice

CHAPTER ONE

Setting the scene

"If you are what you should be, you will set the whole world on fire!"

—Catherine of Siena 1347–1380

The purpose of the book

When in the past I have been asked the question "How do you separate spiritual direction from therapy?", I would try to identify and separate out strands that might belong in therapy but not in spiritual direction, or the other way round. I find I can no longer do this, as I have come to the view that, apart from some of the language that I might intentionally choose to use, the processes are so integrated that they cannot easily be dissected into their constituent parts.

On a number of occasions in the past few years I have been invited to work with groups to explore possible similarities and differences between spiritual direction and therapy. These opportunities have elicited a variety of responses, ranging from "Surely they're both the same?" at one end of the scale to "Surely they're completely different?" at the other. I have been aware that, on occasions, I have faced what felt like hostility from members of both the therapy and the spiritual

1

direction "camps" when attempting to draw parallels and focus on similarities. I have sensed that participants wanted me to stress the differences, inviting me to make a clear and definitive demarcation between the two. This has puzzled me, as it is my belief that the intention of the two activities is the same—to offer a process that can enable our clients or directees to develop, to flourish, to be enriched, to become more the person they are born to be, and, in the broadest sense, to be healed.

Working on the hypothesis that such hostility may well arise out of anxiety, uncertainty, and lack of understanding, this book is an attempt to shine some light on the topic, to give some of the arguments an airing, and, I sincerely hope, to encourage reflection and discussion. I firmly believe that the two traditions have a lot to learn from each other.

All the great world religions have their own rich traditions of spiritual guidance and support, but this book specifically addresses the Christian model of spiritual direction. This is not because I privilege it over that of other faiths, but because it is the one with which I am familiar and in which I am personally involved. I think it is also relevant that psychotherapy seems to have developed and flourished in western countries with a strong Christian history.

I am also aware that, while there is already an enormous body of research and literature about spiritual direction and about psychotherapy—, including a considerable amount that addresses the question of similarities and differences—this has largely originated in north America and thus reflects that particular culture and prevailing practice. At the same time, the literature on all aspects of psychotherapy in the United Kingdom continues to increase—including references to spirituality—but not nearly as much has been published about spiritual direction, and very little on the similarities and differences between the two. The psychotherapy and the spiritual direction communities in the United Kingdom are very different from those in the United States and Canada in terms of professional training and practice, ethical and legal requirements, client expectations, the national culture, and attitudes towards religion and spirituality. With these limitations of literature of a United Kingdom origin, it is inevitable that I shall draw on some north American sources that inform the development of thinking in this country; it is also clear that there are twentieth century contributions to the literature addressing the nature of spiritual direction that are considered to be "classics" in this field. However, there does seem to be a gap—in terms of the examination of current practice and of the relationship between therapy and spiritual direction—and it is my hope that this book may make a contribution towards closing it.

Definitions

In order to explore the differences and similarities between spiritual direction and therapy, it is important to be clear what we mean by such labels and how each of these two traditions identifies itself and what it does. It seems necessary, therefore, to define the terms that will be used throughout this book, although in my exploration of this subject, I have been very aware just how much the limitations of language impede and inhibit my attempts to describe the processes involved in both spiritual direction and psychotherapy. As Corbett says, "The sacred is irreducible" (1996, p. 81), and all our attempts at definitions of what are, at heart, metaphysical and mystical issues must recognise the inherent elements of nuance, mystery, and uncertainty. However, I recognise the importance of establishing some common understanding before going any further.

What is spirituality?

Swinton states very simply: "Spirituality is the outward expression of the inner workings of the human spirit" (2001, p. 20). He then examines the question in considerable depth and asserts that "spirituality can be categorized into two types: non-religious and religious" and identifies the following aspects as the central features of spirituality: "meaning (the ontological significance of life); value (beliefs and standards); transcendence (expanding self-boundaries); connecting (relationships with self, other, God/higher power and the environment); becoming (an unfolding of life that demands reflection and experience)" (ibid., pp. 23–25). Thorne suggests that "the very word 'spiritual' is commonly used by those who wish to affirm their belief in an overarching reality which points to the interconnectedness of the created order and to a perception of the human being as essentially mysterious and not ultimately definable in biological, psychological or sociological terms" (2002, p. 6) and Gubi states: "Spirituality is ultimately about the search for meaning and fulfilment in life … Spirituality includes a sense of transcendence—the experience and appreciation of a dimension beyond self which can lead to expanding self-boundaries" (2010, p. 8).

All the above statements attempt to define a significant interior experience that links us as individuals to something outside of and greater than ourselves, and which we recognise through personal experience.

What is religion?

The Oxford Dictionary (2001) definition is as follows: "1. The belief in and worship of a superhuman controlling power, especially of a personal god or gods, a particular system of faith and worship; 2. A pursuit or interest followed with devotion." However, Swinton (2001) suggests that spirituality may be religious or non-religious and Thorne asserts that religion and spirituality are not by definition connected (2002, p. 6). Swinton further cites Allport and Ross' work on intrinsic and extrinsic religiousness; intrinsic religious faith offers a framework for understanding and making meaning of life, whereas extrinsic faith offers a more utilitarian and less altruistic religious world view. "In theological terms the extrinsic type turns to but without turning away from self" (1967, p. 434).

Richards & Bergin address the interrelatedness of religion and spirituality as follows:

> Religion has to do with theistic beliefs, practices, and feelings that are often, but not always, expressed institutionally and denominationally as well as personally. Thus, the terms *religious* and *spiritual* are interrelated, but they can be distinguished from each other along several dimensions. Religious expressions tend to be denominational, external, cognitive, behavioural, ritualistic, and public. Spiritual experiences tend to be universal, ecumenical, internal, affective, spontaneous, and private. It is possible to be religious without being spiritual and spiritual without being religious. (1997, p. 13)

That there is a difference between religion and spirituality is further evidenced by the fact that organised religion, in the shape of formalised church communities, is not necessarily the place to which people turn when looking for spiritual direction. It is interesting to note that many spiritual directors are not connected to a church in any formalised way—and some may have little or no connection—which would seem to raise questions about the nature of the spiritual support that many churches are in fact offering.

What is psychotherapy?

If we go back to the roots of the word "psychotherapy" we see that it comes from the Greek words "psyche", meaning the breath of life, and "therapeia," meaning attendant or servant. West (2004, p. 144) suggests that one translation of the word "psychotherapist" would be "soul attender".

However, the United Kingdom Council for Psychotherapy (UKCP) more formally defines psychotherapy as follows: "Psychotherapy aims to help clients gain insight into their difficulties or distress, establish a greater understanding of their motivation, and enables them to find more appropriate ways of coping or bring about changes in their thinking and behaviour"; and also explains that "Psychotherapy involves exploring feelings, *beliefs,* thoughts and relevant events, sometimes from childhood and personal history, in a structured way with someone trained to help you do it safely" (www.psychotherapy.org.uk, italics mine), thus clearly indicating that addressing *beliefs* may be part of therapy.

Traditionally, and in some cases currently, some psychotherapists might not consider the client's spirituality as relevant, and may even see it is a sign of pathology. However, approaches to therapy that are defined specifically as "transpersonal" (for example, psychosynthesis) seek to acknowledge, yet move beyond, the awareness of the individual self as a separate, isolated consciousness. Grof and Grof define the word transpersonal as "transcending the usual way of perceiving and interpreting the world" (1989, p. 7) and Clarkson (1995, p. 7) includes the transpersonal as a modality in her examination of the therapeutic relationship.

What is spiritual direction?

The term "spiritual direction" is, perhaps, an unfortunate one, implying that the relationship is an unequal one in which the power is vested in one participant who gives advice and guidance, is directive, and who tells the other what to do and, possibly even in some circumstances, what to think.

In reality, the relationship in spiritual direction is ideally one of mutuality in which the director places himself or herself alongside the directee and is a companion on the spiritual journey, seeking to explore and deepen the relationship with God. The tradition of spiritual direction suggests that it is the Holy Spirit—seen as a third presence in the room—who is the director, not the person whom the directee has come to see. This is in line with the opening sentence of *Spiritual Friendship* by Aelred of Riveaulx: "Here we are, you and I, and I hope a third, Christ, is in our midst" (1974 p. 51). Thus spiritual direction is often seen as a triadic relationship rather than a dyadic one.

Benner defines spiritual direction as follows: "Spiritual direction is a prayer process in which a person seeking help in cultivating a deeper personal relationship with God meets with another for prayer and conversation that is focused on increasing awareness of God in the midst of life experiences" (2002, p. 94) which, by including the words "in the midst of life experiences", acknowledges the "groundedness" of the process, suggesting that this is no airy-fairy business, but relates to the everyday life of the individual. Directees bring themselves in their entirety into direction, not just their "God bit". Benner, referring to spiritual directors, continues: "... the essence of their role is discernment—or better, co-discernment" (ibid., p. 205), with its suggestion of mutuality and shared intention.

Jones defines spiritual direction as follows: "Spiritual direction is a relationship entered into with another under mutual obedience to the revelation of God in Christ" (1982, p. 4) which, by referring to mutual obedience, implies that there is no sense of inequality.

Merton wrote: "The whole purpose of spiritual direction is to penetrate beneath the surface of a man's life, to get behind the facade of conventional gestures and attitudes which he presents to the world, and to bring out his inner spiritual freedom, which is what we call the likeness of Christ in his soul" (1960, p. 16). Here Merton is commenting on the actual process of direction, on what is happening in the sacred space co-created by director and directee.

Barry and Connelly define spiritual direction as "... help given by one Christian to another which enables that person ... to respond to God, to grow in intimacy with God and to live out the consequences" (1984, p. 8). I would suggest that in "living out the consequences" we could also very well be describing the outcome of therapy. Birmingham and Connolly comment on the purpose of spiritual direction when they write: "Spiritual direction places itself at the service of the relationship between the directee and God and of the development of the relationship that God has put underway" (1994, p. 51).

In some circles, preferred terms include spiritual accompanier, soul friend, or companion, and, while I am in great sympathy with the desire to move away from the idea of a power-based relationship in which there is an expectation that one person will take a "directive" approach towards the other, personally I find that my default term is spiritual director. This isn't accidental or merely out of habit, but rather from an appreciation of the long historical tradition of spiritual direction. I very much value the connection and continuity with this long and historical tradition—the sense of standing on giants' shoulders when reflecting on the practice of spiritual direction in the twenty-first century. Nevertheless, I understand and sympathise with the reluctance that many have to using this term.

Similar or different?

When reflecting on similarities and differences, I come back to the principle already mentioned that spiritual direction is a triadic rather than dyadic relationship. I do not necessarily see that this is different in the therapeutic relationship. While many therapists may find it an unacceptable notion, I am sure that there will be those who would claim to be aware of the presence of God in their clinical work.

May, psychiatrist and spiritual director, gives the following description of how he sees the role of therapist and director:

> In humanistic therapy one could say "I bring all that I am into this relationship with you. For the time we are together, I attend to you with all my heart and with all my expertise. I give my attention to our being together in the hope that this will facilitate your growth and health ...." In spiritual direction one might say "My prayers are for God's will to be done in you and for your constant depending in God. During this time that we are together I give myself, my awareness and attention and hopes and heart to God for you. I surrender myself to God for your sake." (1992, p. 120)

I would suggest that "I give my attention to our being together in the hope that this will facilitate your growth and health" could very easily be translated as "I surrender myself to God for your sake" and, even if there are certain nuances that differentiate these two statements, the primary and underlying message from director to directee is identical to that from therapist to client, that is, "I am fully present in the service of your well-being".

Similarly Edwards states:

> We go to a counsellor to try to gain insight and greater flexibility related to the way we function in daily living. A divine force may be accepted in the relationship, but the primary intent of paying attention to that force is to use it to help us improve our personal effectiveness. In spiritual direction the focus is on the divine force, on God, as the integral core of our being and purpose. We go to a spiritual director because we want to become more attuned to God's Spirit in our spirit and freely live out of divine love. (2001, p. 24)

My experience leads me to the conclusion that, for Christians, these two statements overlap and interweave, that they cannot be divided quite as simply as Edwards perhaps suggests. For people of sincere faith, everything in life is infused with God's spirit, and the desire to live out of divine love is central to all aspects of life. As Ball says: "To accompany a person on their journey of faith … is to be concerned with every aspect of that person's being … It is concerned with helping them to apply their faith in the context of the society and the relationships in which they are set" (1996, p. 42).

Who am I? Psychotherapist or spiritual director?

Our journeys are all unique, and we find ourselves at a particular place, at any given time, as a result of our personal life experience. Perhaps it is therefore relevant for me to describe briefly the background that has influenced and informed my own journey, and to outline how my work as therapist and as spiritual director has become so intertwined.

With the perfect vision of hindsight, I can see now that there was something inexorable about the progress of my life in terms of both faith and career, and how, very unexpectedly, these two journeys towards becoming a psychotherapist and a spiritual director converged and began to be mutually integrated.

I was brought up in a tiny hamlet in rural Worcestershire by a devout Anglican mother, my father showing little interest in matters of faith, and my life as a child very much centred on the parish church. I am very aware of the influence this early experience of church had on me, as I accepted both faith and practice pretty much unquestioningly until well into adult life as a married woman and the mother of two young daughters. It was at this stage that a sequence of events and influences caused me to examine what I believed, and I had to face up to the fact that I could no longer trust in the certainties to which I had previously held so firmly—all of which led me to the conclusion that I needed to re-evaluate every aspect of my life.

One of the results of this re-evaluation was that I became much less involved in church activities and began training to teach in further education. On completing the course I got a job teaching business studies—and so my 25- year-long career as a teacher in the "second chance" sector of education began. Having taught for many years, I signed up for a course leading to a Masters in Post Compulsory Education, and chose counselling as a module, thinking that it would be useful in my role as course tutor. And then I was hooked! This module reawakened my belief that it is in relationships that learning and change can take place, something which I had passionately believed when I started teaching, but which had become submerged in the prevailing culture which gave primacy to performance criteria and behavioural outcomes. I began to feel alive again.

The module served as an effective "taster" and I subsequently joined a part-time counselling diploma course which I very much enjoyed, particularly the experiential process which gave me permission to explore my own story and personal development, something which my typically Protestant background would previously have considered at best rather self-indulgent and at worst totally self-absorbed. But even before the course had finished I knew that it wasn't going to be enough; I wanted to know more, I wanted to stay in training, I wanted to have my own therapy—and above all I wanted to find some way of integrating my Christian faith into all that I was learning.

My desire to find a way in which these two strands could be integrated authentically became central to my thinking. I did not want to ignore my faith while I studied psychological theory, but I also wanted to immerse myself in sound research-based therapeutic knowledge. I was determined to find a way in which the two could co-exist so that I could develop as the psychotherapist that I firmly believed God wanted me to become. Yet I did not see the label "Christian counsellor" fitting with my personal beliefs. So I set out to track down a training programme that would allow me to explore both strands of my passion simultaneously; and it was also at this time that I first engaged with my own therapy and my own spiritual direction.

During the next rigorous six years of training, clinical practice, supervision, and personal therapy, there were many times when I wondered whether I had bitten off more than I could chew but I was always confident that I had chosen the right training programme. Whether this was because of, or despite, the challenges it raised I was never too sure! Part of this process of challenge was to recognise that I had to examine all my beliefs if I were to emerge as an authentic and integrated therapist, but I never felt that my Christian faith was under attack, only that I was being invited to be completely honest with myself and to explore in depth how my integrative model could accommodate my personal belief system. I was, however, sometimes aware of a degree of scepticism from my fellow students and this scepticism also provided a catalyst for further examination of my core beliefs.

At the same time I enrolled on a spiritual direction training programme. So, for the first two years, the spiritual direction course ran concurrently with the psychotherapy training, a situation which brought its own challenges in terms of emotional resilience, intellectual resources, and spiritual discernment, not to mention time management. However, it also meant that I was developing my knowledge and skills in the two disciplines simultaneously, which I hoped would result in a level of natural integration right from the beginning. While there were times when I wondered whether I was mad to be doing both courses at the same time, with hindsight I can see the benefits of my decision in terms of both personal and professional integration.

Having completed these trainings, I began to practise as both a spiritual director and a psychotherapist and was often very aware just how much the two overlapped. The general wisdom at the time seemed to be that there were great differences, which meant that I faced quite a struggle as I endeavoured to conceptualise for myself just what these differences were. As already mentioned, traditional thinking suggested that a meeting between director and directee is in the presence of the Holy Spirit, for Whom the director becomes a channel. However, as I developed as a director and as a psychotherapist, I began to question this way of conceptualising the process: my experience with directees was identical to that with clients, in that I felt there were moments when we were relating with each other at what therapists would identify as relational depth and which, in another language, might be described as the Christ in me meeting the Christ in the other. For many Christian therapists, this triangular model, traditionally accepted in the practice of spiritual direction, can be just as relevant in the therapeutic setting, resonating with Buber's (1923) concept of mutuality in the I-Thou encounter, which will be explored further in Chapter Seven.

As my training continued, I was coming to an awareness of just how much psychotherapy and spiritual direction have in common, despite some differences in the nature of the material that was brought by clients or directees. For some time I also identified the purpose of the two activities as different: I saw the process of therapy as being largely about problem solving, personal growth, or making meaning; while spiritual direction was about the individual's relationship with God, their prayer life, and their spiritual journey. However, gradually, I came to realise just how much the purposes overlap as well. If some-one's faith is central, then how they solve problems or make meaning of their life will inevitably be predicated on their relationship with God and will involve their prayer life, thus becoming part of their spiritual journey. And even when working with people for whom any notion of spirituality or religious belief was absent or possibly alien, *my* faith was still part of the equation, even when unknown to the client.

As my ideas and understanding developed out of my increased awareness of the process involved in both psychotherapy and spiritual direction, I became less and less sure about the differences that I had previously accepted and avowed. I came to see these differences as being much more about language, and the way in which it is used, than about anything substantive. I also realised that it was not difficult to move from one language to another. Just as I would seek to be attuned to individual therapy clients and would thus pay careful attention to their choice of language and vocabulary, similarly I would be seeking a deep mutual connection and recognition with individual directees. In most cases I could move between languages without difficulty and, when a problem of understanding arose, I would check out what was meant in exactly the same way as in any other psychotherapeutic relationship.

Motivation is also a relevant question. While for some the purpose of therapy may be personal development, for most there is at least an element of dissatisfaction with life, and many present in crisis.

The initial motivation for seeking spiritual direction is almost invariably a desire to explore the directee's spiritual journey although this may in fact hide an underlying need for therapy. In some circles, particularly amongst clergy, having a spiritual director is seen as "acceptable"—not necessarily the case with having a therapist. It is common to receive an initial request for spiritual direction, only to realise almost immediately that what is really being sought (either consciously or unconsciously) is therapy. Many people still hold negative perceptions about receiving therapy and this attitude may be exaggerated for some Christians, many of whom hold the view that their faith should provide sufficient support in all circumstances.

Who is this book for?

So, who might find this book interesting or useful; who might be drawn to explore this subject? I hope that it might be of interest to anyone involved in any way in either psychotherapy or spiritual direction, that is to say, psychotherapists and counsellors, spiritual directors, supervisors and trainers in both disciplines, medical practitioners and those engaged in the field of mental health, managers of agencies and other therapeutic settings, clergy, chaplains, and pastoral workers—and I would certainly include anyone at all who is interested in exploring their own psychological and spiritual journey.

There is considerable evidence that the issue of spirituality has recently become more mainstream in therapy and this evidence will be examined in Chapter Three. Similarly, some spiritual direction courses are beginning to address psychological issues as part of the curriculum. This would indicate that there is a desire for greater mutual understanding, and I hope that anyone who shares this desire will find this book relevant to their work. My aim is that practitioners may become confident enough to explore what is within their limits of competence and, when relevant, able to make an appropriate referral.

Summary of chapters to follow

I am very conscious that not every chapter will be of interest to all readers, some of whom may well prefer to select what seems relevant to them and their own situation or work. It therefore seems helpful to give some clue about the content of each of the following chapters.

Chapter Two will explore the early roots and influences that I consider are shared by psychotherapy and spiritual direction and from which each has developed in its individual way. It will be seen that they have much in common in terms of traditions and practices and just how much psychological understanding and insight is demonstrated in the work of spiritual directors from the third to the twenty-first centuries.

Chapter Three looks at attitudes to spirituality in therapy, both in the past and the present, and discusses the advantages of encouraging therapists to integrate this subject into their work with clients. Similarly, Chapter Four will examine how spiritual directors can be aware of psychological issues in their work, including unconscious process and psychosis, risk assessment, and when and how to refer clients for medical intervention. Similarities and differences between depression and "Dark Night of the Soul" experiences will be explored in Chapter Five.

Out of the material in the above chapters, many legal and ethical questions will be identified and these will be the subject of Chapter Six, leading into an examination in Chapter Seven of the question of power in therapeutic and spiritual direction relationships, possible origins and causes, and how these are maintained in current practice. In exploring the whole subject of ethical and competent practice, the question of whether prayer can ever be considered to have a place in therapy, and how this may differ in spiritual direction, becomes evident and this is the subject of Chapter Eight.

Chapter Nine will start with a brief "snapshot" of how spirituality is currently viewed in psychotherapy training programmes in the United Kingdom and how psychological issues are being addressed on spiritual direction courses. This will lead to reflection on what improvements might be made in both areas in order to increase confidence and competence in practitioners in both fields.

In Chapter Ten the evidence for the differences and similarities between psychotherapy and spiritual direction will be drawn together and challenges to both will be considered. The possibly heretical question of whether spiritual direction might be seen as a specific modality of psychotherapy will be discussed, with reference to Frank and Frank's Common Factors Theory and to the debate about whether psychotherapy is better defined by title or by function.

Taking a holistic approach, I therefore suggest that, if we focus too much on which bit is therapy and which bit is spiritual direction, we are in danger of missing the essence and purpose of what we are doing. While there may be differences between the two activities in terms of practical, boundary, and ethical issues such as payment, insurance and confidentiality, I would argue that the process is essentially the same and this is the case that I present in the chapters that follow.

CHAPTER TWO

A common heritage?

"What has been will be again
What has been done will be done again;
There is nothing new under the sun"

—Ecclesiastes 1:9

In this chapter I shall offer a brief historical overview of the origins of both spiritual direction and psychotherapy, together with the development of therapy in the twentieth and twenty-first centuries. I shall suggest that there currently seems to be increasing convergence between therapy and spiritual direction and shall examine the similarities and differences that are emerging.

Historical overview

As mentioned in the previous chapter, I very much value the sense of historical continuity that I experience when I call myself a spiritual director, rather than any of the other terms that have some currency at the moment, such as spiritual accompanier or soul friend. I suggest that this may be because the roots of the practice of therapy are grounded in the same traditions as those found in spiritual direction.

15

The following brief overview of the origins and development of spiritual direction and of therapy, from the beginning of the Christian era to twenty-first century psychotherapy, via the Age of Enlightenment, is necessarily a selective summary and is not an attempt at an exhaustive record. It will show a consistent thread of one-to-one relationships throughout the centuries, relationships that have provided much valued spiritual and psychological support in all sorts of circumstances and contexts.

It is worth considering whether the different "schools" of therapy (that is, psychodynamic, humanistic, and cognitive behavioural) have unconsciously absorbed teaching and wisdom from the traditions of Christianity and, if so, how this affects therapeutic attitudes and practice today. How much of a heritage do spiritual direction and modern therapy share, and how can both traditions be encouraged and enabled to acknowledge and value common ground where it exists?

Origins of spiritual direction

While the term "Talking Cure" is usually attributed to Freud and his colleagues working at the end of the nineteenth/beginning of the twentieth centuries, the practice of engaging in one-to-one dialogue with someone willing and able to take a dispassionate view is not new. There have been numerous examples throughout history, with a particular tradition in the Christian church and in other major faiths.

It could be said that St Paul was the first spiritual director, using the medium of letters to offer support and spiritual accompaniment to seekers through his many epistles. Subsequently, in the third and fourth centuries AD, seekers, whom we now know as the desert fathers and mothers, withdrew to the deserts of Egypt, Palestine, and Syria in order to live a life of solitude and to find God. They often formed groups centred around a leader, thus founding something akin to the first monastic communities. The leaders of these communities took on the role of teacher, which gives us an early model of what would become known as spiritual directors.

Amongst these leaders was St Anthony, often considered to be the founder of Christian monasticism, who withdrew from the world around AD270. After about 15 years he retired and lived in complete solitude for 20 years without seeing anyone, food being thrown to him over the wall which separated him from the world. Pilgrims visited him, but initially he refused to see them, until a colony of ascetics formed around his dwelling and eventually he engaged with them as their spiritual leader.

Evagrius of Pontus (AD345–399) was influential in establishing an approach to Christian spiritual practice and also in identifying what he called "Eight Deadly Thoughts", which he proposed had the potential to lead to unhealthy and unhelpful attachments or even addiction, thus linking disordered thoughts to negative and destructive behaviours. As Nelson comments:

> Over 1500 years before Freud, Evagrius developed a sophisticated understanding of the relationship between desire, depression, and anger. He saw that unhealthy attachments and frustration of desire could lead to depression or anxiety. He viewed anger as an outgrowth of depression, although on occasion anger could also lead to depression as when thoughts of revenge go unfulfilled. (2009, p. 362)

John Cassian (AD360–435) introduced the ideas of the desert fathers and mothers to Western Christianity, establishing monasteries in the south of France. He was particularly interested in the imagery of dreams and sought evidence of what he called "unconscious maladies of the soul". Both Evagrius and Cassian viewed Christianity as a way of life that integrated all aspects of human experience. While it might perhaps be overstating the case to suggest that their work prefigured that of Freud and the psychoanalysts, it is certainly a reminder that the heritage of therapy has a rich and varied history.

The writings of St Francis of Assisi, Thomas à Kempis, and St Frances de Sales all offer guidance in spiritual formation, and of particular relevance to twentieth/twenty-first century psychological thinking is the legacy of St Ignatius of Loyola (AD1491–1556). In his early adult years, Ignatius lived the life of a courtier and soldier in Spain and his expectation was that this lifestyle would continue into later life. However, after being wounded in battle at the age of 26, in 1517 at Pamplona, he experienced a religious conversion and founded the Society of Jesus, or Jesuits. His wisdom resulted in others joining him and the development of what we know as the "Spiritual Exercises" (Fleming, 1996).

These Exercises provide a framework for meditating on Biblical passages or Christian themes in order to increase self-awareness, together with models and methods of discernment for decision making which offer us practical ways of problem solving that are still relevant today. They are undertaken with a spiritual director, who helps directees to reflect on their deepest desires in order to identify and explore what will lead to authentic inner freedom. It can be argued that the focus and activities of the Exercises have much in common with recognised therapeutic techniques, for example, the use of multisensory imagination to enhance the felt experience rather than relying purely on cognitive forms of understanding. The regular practice of the *daily examen*, or reflection on the events of the day, is also central to the Spiritual Exercises, with a view to monitoring our actions and encounters in order to grow more Christ-like. While the motivation may be rather different, we can nevertheless see parallels in psychotherapy, such as identifying what helps and what hinders, and cost/benefit analysis in working towards change.

Ignatius clearly recognised the importance of acknowledging the different elements by which we make sense of our experience, which, without privileging one over another, he expresses succinctly in his prayer "Take, Lord, and receive all my liberty, my memory, my understanding and my entire will" (Fleming, 1996, p. 177), offering an holistic view of the human person that resonates with our understanding today. He clearly understood the need for self-acceptance and the damaging effects of low self-esteem, while not denying the sinful nature of the human condition. Ignatian spirituality thus offers us many examples of knowledge and insight into the inner world which have considerable resonances with psychological theory today.

Notable examples of fine writing in English from the middle ages are by the unknown author of *The Cloud of Unknowing* (2001) and Dame Julian of Norwich, who wrote *Revelations of Divine Love* (2003), both of whom have considerable influence on spiritual thinking in the twenty-first century.

Writings from sixteenth century Spain by St Teresa of Avila and St John of the Cross, both active spiritual directors, show considerable understanding of psychological matters. In fact May, a psychiatrist, states: "Teresa's psychological insights compare favourably with those of Freud and his twentieth-century followers. John's descriptions of attachment brilliantly enhance modern addiction theory" (2004, p. 38). Their writings in relation to Dark Night of the Soul experiences are examined in Chapter Five.

John Pierre de Caussade, born in Toulouse in 1675, is also a significant figure. A Jesuit priest, he became spiritual director to the order of the Sisters of the Visitation in Nancy. His teaching about "the sacrament of the present moment" emphasises the importance of living fully in the here-and-now, which has resonances with the practice of mindfulness meditation that is currently being incorporated into many therapeutic models, particularly for managing depression and anxiety.

We can also see examples of the practice of spiritual direction by the Protestant reformers—Luther, Zwingli, and Calvin, amongst others—who offered support and encouragement through their writing, so the tradition is by no means exclusive to the Roman Catholic tradition. In the Anglican tradition, there are those known collectively as "the Caroline Divines", a group which includes Thomas Ken, George Herbert, Lancelot Andrewes, and Jeremy Taylor, who still influence views on spirituality today. Ball tells us that Taylor "charged the clergy … to 'exhort' their people … to a conversation with their minister in spiritual things" (1996, p. 17)—which sounds like a call to spiritual direction to me!

At the beginning of the twentieth century, Friedrich von Hugel, Rudolph Otto, William James, and others were showing great interest in the links and overlaps between psychology and religion and, in England, Evelyn Underhill and Reginald Somerset Ward are notable spiritual directors.

Other examples of where the ideas and practice of spiritual direction and therapy merge can be seen in a constant theme that emerges from many of the writings on spiritual development, which propose that following an intentional spiritual practice results in letting go of attachments and in the development of a sense of inner peace—what we might call the emergence of the true self. It is interesting to note that Winnicott (1975) and Merton (1961)—the former an English psychologist, the latter an American Trappist monk—both address the question of the false self and seek to address how the true self can be revealed. Nelson describes the false self as consisting of

> superficial or illusionary ideas about ourselves and the pattern of behaviour we mistakenly believe to be essential to us … The false self is not free; it fragments us and puts us at odds with reality, others and our self; because of this, it produces a general feeling of dread, guilt, or anxiety … The true self is hidden under this false exterior. (2009, p. 445)

Nelson also comments that "early Christian writers reject the idea that mind and body can be separated ... we are a composite of body and soul that are separate in nature but interpenetrate (*perichoresis*) so that they are intimately related and actively reciprocal" (ibid., pp. 438–439). He refers to experimental research indicating that the production of certain brain chemicals involved in addictions is reduced by prayer, fasting, and other ascetic practices. These practices have much in common with those associated with mindfulness in supporting and maintaining good mental health, for example, improved mood and a sense of inner well-being and freedom, which are reflected in the state known as *hesychia*, or a sense of inner peace and connection with God.

There would seem to be considerable evidence that there have always been people who, although they did not use the psychological language of today, recognised and described the psychological experiences they observed—and found ways of working with them from within a spiritual frame of reference. As West interestingly points out, "the decline in clergy and church workers has been paralleled by an equivalent increase in social workers and therapists" (2000, p. 18). So perhaps we might even consider that the psychologists of the twentieth century were the newcomers to territory that had already been mapped by their religious predecessors, and it therefore seems relevant to consider the origins and development of the professional practice of psychotherapy.

Origins and development of psychotherapy

Current practice identifies three main "schools" of psychotherapy: psychodynamic, humanistic, and cognitive/behavioural. While there are many variations within these schools, they are nevertheless identifiable by certain basic principles which inform theory and practice.

Psychodynamic school

Opinions vary about the precise dates of the cultural movement that has become known as "The Age of Enlightenment" which started around the end of the seventeenth/beginning of the eighteenth century. It is during this period that questions of religion and philosophy began to be seen in the light of an increasingly "scientific" framework, a framework offering the ideas of rationalism and positivism that Freud was to find so attractive. So it is perhaps at this point in history that the common heritage of therapy and spiritual direction begin to diverge, at least for some time to come.

The Victorians believed that the body, rather than the mind, held the answer to psychological problems. Freud, a neurologist by profession, along with his colleague Joseph Breuer, adopted what he called the "talking cure" in Vienna at the end of the nineteenth century, forming the foundations of what would become known as the psychodynamic school of therapy.

Freud is known for psychoanalysis, which is based on the importance of unconscious process, defences, neurosis, dreams, sexuality, etc. Coming from a medical background, he referred to those with whom he worked as "patients". Others subsequently revised and developed his ideas and today many psychodynamic practitioners would call themselves post-Freudian, with an emphasis on relationships, not only external, with others (intersubjective), but also internal, within ourselves (intrapsychic), in terms of different aspects of the Self. The work of Jung, Adler, Klein, and Winnicott, among others, also comes within the psychodynamic school, in which the emphasis is on how patterns from the past affect the present and the future and where the therapist offers interpretations of the presented material.

In a sense Freud considers the possibility that God exists but argues that this is highly unlikely and justifies his conclusion that the believer is "defending a lost cause" (Palmer 1997, p. 80).

Jung's experience, however, was different and he famously said "Believe? I don't believe, I *know*". For Jung, it was the absence of religion, rather than its presence, that is a symptom of neurosis. Other practitioners within the psychodynamic school—including, among others, Erikson (1968), Guntrip (1957), and Winnicott (1975)—express views that demonstrate their personal religious beliefs and faith.

Humanistic school

It is in what is known as the Humanistic School of psychotherapy that we begin to see a reconnection between spiritual direction and therapy in terms of a holistic approach to exploring inner healing and growth. A number of therapies are included in the Humanistic school: for example, Person-centred therapy, Gestalt therapy, Transactional

Analysis, and Psychosynthesis (this latter offering perhaps the most overtly spiritual or religious model of all the mainstream therapies). Integrative models of therapy are also classified as Humanistic, in which therapists develop their own framework, including theory, skills, and techniques from a number of traditions.

Client-centred, or person-centred, therapy originated in the United States with the work of Carl Rogers, the son of a pastor, who was initially training to become a church minister. However, on a trip to China in 1922 he was exposed to the ideas of the progressive education movement, which emphasised a trust in the individual child's innate ability to learn. He also became more aware of ideas from other faiths and, as a result, decided to train as a clinical psychologist, working mainly with disturbed children and their families. He observed that clients gained the greatest benefit in therapy when they are allowed to find their own solutions—a strong reminder of the discernment processes advocated by St Ignatius of Loyola in the fifteenth century. Clients are the experts on themselves and the counsellor, taking a holistic approach, maintains a non-directive stance.

Rogers also believed that, as human beings, we all have what he called a "self-actualising tendency" (1951), that is, an innate quality to develop and grow in order to reach our potential. He believed that his work as a counsellor depended on what he called the core conditions—the ability of the counsellor to offer empathy and unconditional positive regard to clients and to be real, or congruent, in this relationship. Rogers proposed that these conditions were both sufficient and necessary for a beneficial outcome to the work. He later wrote on the subject of "presence", by which he meant the potential for healing in the profound relationship between client and therapist. While acknowledging that patterns from the past affect the present, in person-centred therapy the emphasis is often on motivation and initiating the process of change.

The cognitive and behavioural therapy school (CBT)

(Cognitive behavioural therapy, cognitive analytic therapy, rational emotive behaviour therapy, multi-modal therapy)

Aaron Beck, Albert Ellis, and Arnold Lazarus are names particularly associated with the development of therapies in the cognitive and behavioural school. These therapies share the belief that when we hold unrealistic or negative beliefs about ourselves or our experiences, emotional distress will follow. It is our response to activating events, rather than the events themselves, that causes this emotional upset. By identifying what our negative automatic thoughts are, we can learn a new internal dialogue and develop the skills necessary to make changes in our thinking. West (2000, pp. 39–43) gives examples of Buddhist strategies that are consistent with modern cognitive behavioural techniques, drawing our attention to the fact that it is not only the Christian church that has offered us a tradition of addressing psychological issues.

CBT is the therapy of choice under the government initiative Increasing Access to Psychological Therapies (IAPT). However, techniques, skills, and strategies may be adopted by practitioners from other schools for specific areas of work.

A common heritage?

There seem to be many similarities between what has been offered by spiritual directors over the centuries and what therapists have been offering in the past one hundred years. Both spiritual direction and therapy attempt to address philosophical and existential issues that are central to the world view of individuals who are asking questions and attempting to make meaning of their personal life experience. However, rather than acknowledging common areas of interest and practice, psychotherapists and spiritual directors have in the past often been suspicious of each others' work.

Similar or different?

It is apparent that spiritual writers of previous centuries show evidence of sophisticated psychological insight. The context in which they were living and working may be very different from our own, and the language obviously reflects the thinking of their time, but they instinctively seem to be aware of what therapists sometimes labour to learn today. It is interesting to note that methods and techniques used in the past, for example, the need to seek out someone to talk to, the use of guided imagery, cost/benefit analysis—all of which can be found in the Spiritual Exercises of St Ignatius—resonate with modern therapeutic practice: just as human nature does not change, elements of wise and effective practice can be observed consistently through the centuries. Our understanding of why and how these methods and strategies are effective may increase over time, particularly with the development of neuroscience, but their inherent effectiveness had been recognised long before the twenty-first century.

And why should we be surprised by this? Why should we think that it is only our generation that has such insight and awareness? The heritage that therapists and spiritual directors share is a precious resource that both should value—and, I would suggest, there is more that unites them than divides them.

CHAPTER THREE

Spiritual issues in therapy: the hidden ingredient?

"Among all my patients in the second half of life—that is over 35—there has not been one whose problem in the last resort was not that of finding a religious outlook on life ...."

—Jung (*Modern Man in Search of a Soul* 1933)

Introduction

If you've had therapy, I wonder whether you raised spiritual matters—or did you deliberately avoid any mention of your faith or beliefs? In this chapter I shall look at attitudes to the inclusion of spirituality in therapy, historically and today, and the potential benefits of integration. I shall examine examples of specific circumstances and contexts where spiritual issues are more likely to be the focus of the therapy and which may lead to particular ethical dilemmas. I shall also consider the effect that addressing spiritual views in therapy may have on therapists, and the question of referring clients for spiritual direction will be raised.

Attitudes to spirituality in therapy: historically and today

The question of the nature and significance of spiritual issues in therapy has been around as long as therapy itself. As we have seen in the previous chapter, Freud, influenced as he was by the Age of Enlightenment and committed to seeing therapy as a science and free from church control, considered religious commitment to be neurotic and illusory, pathological and unhelpful. However, as Nelson (2009, p. *vii*) points out, many of Freud's ideas are not actually supported by any empirical evidence that would be considered satisfactory by today's scientists. As we have also seen, Jung maintained that religious issues were central to all his clients over thirty-five years of age and above his front door was carved *"Vocatus atque non vocatus, deus aderit"*, which means "Whether called or not, God will be present".

Experience may suggest that historically, and perhaps as part of Freud's legacy, many therapists have taken a somewhat unsympathetic or even hostile attitude towards faith and religion and that this may be the result of the perceived split between what is considered to be scientific and what is not. It seems paradoxical that a subject that holds such great importance for so many clients is often seen at best to be "out of bounds" and at worst to be pathological. Even in the United States, where religious allegiance is more mainstream than in the United Kingdom, Griffith and Griffith state that "the majority of mental health professionals, with the notable exception of pastoral counsellors, have struggled to find a proper place for people's spiritual lives" (2002, p. 5).

However, writing in a UK context, Culliford states: "Spirituality is universal, unique to every person. It is essentially unifying and involves everyone, including those who do not believe in God or a 'higher being'", and he continues: "Spirituality is thus supraordinate to, and an integrating force for, the other hierarchically arranged dimensions of human life: physical, biological, psychological and psychosocial" (2007, p. 212).

Clarkson (1995) also acknowledges the importance of the spiritual in therapy, which she labels as transpersonal. In her examination of the facets that contribute to the therapeutic relationship, she proposes a model consisting of five modalities: the working alliance; the transferential/countertransferential; the reparative/developmentally needed; the person-to-person; and the transpersonal. In describing the transpersonal modality, Clarkson writes about "the timeless facet of the therapeutic relationship, which is impossible to describe, but refers to the spiritual dimension of the healing relationship" (1995, p. 181). She goes on to invite all therapists, whatever their belief system, to engage in this dimension by saying, "You can explore this dimension without necessarily affirming the existence or truth of the phenomena" (ibid., p. 183).

In the initial meeting with clients, therapists may ask about all sorts of things—family background, employment, past and present relationships, general health, likes and dislikes, hobbies and interests, as well as previous experience of therapy. During this process a great deal of information is gathered—but how often are questions that focus on the spiritual aspects of our clients' lives included? Certainly my own therapist did not enquire about my faith or beliefs in our early sessions and when I started working with clients in the 1990s, I would not have included such questions in my initial intake procedure.

If we enquire quite generally about what helps and supports clients, their response may—or intentionally may not—include reference to spiritual issues, their belief or faith, spiritual practices, or belonging to a faith community. As a result of their research into adult spirituality in Britain, Hay and Hunt note that "very often people would only start to share their spiritual intuitions very late on in a research conversation, once they had judged that it was safe to do so. The taboo arises from two kinds of fears; firstly that they will be targeted by evangelists, secondly they fear being laughed at" (2002, p. 6). Similarly, clients may be anxious that faith issues will be considered pathological if brought to therapy. Jenkins (in West) reports on the experience of a patient in a psychiatric unit who, having raised the subject of a sense of God, was told by other patients, "Don't talk about that stuff in here … you'll never get out" (2001, p. 29). Thus they learnt "to play the game".

It seems therefore that, in the absence of direct questioning, clients may well be reluctant to volunteer information about their faith because they fear that this may be considered part of their "problem" rather than something that may potentially make a positive contribution to a successful therapeutic outcome. A directee of mine (a priest in the Anglican church) told me of an example of such a lack of willingness to engage in this area of human experience. She had previously been referred by her GP to a cognitive-behavioural (CBT) therapist who, in their first session together, actually stated that she would not be willing to work with anything spiritual and suggested that she find somewhere else for this part of the work, as a result of which she had contacted me with spiritual direction in mind. Considering her profession, the CBT therapist's response seemed insensitive at best and positively detrimental at worst.

I find it interesting that some therapists admit to a reluctance to include issues of spirituality into their work, whereas in the case of any other subject they might well be willing to develop their knowledge and understanding by reading, taking part in workshops, attending training courses, or engaging in extra supervision. They would, at least, be prepared to ask relevant questions of their clients in the interests of becoming better informed, and therefore more effective, practitioners, or they might well consider exploring an appropriate referral with their clients. As Pargament states:

> No decent clinician avoids the most private and sensitive of topics; love, sex, death, jealousy, violence, addictions, and betrayal are grist for the therapist's mill. Questions about spirituality and religion, however, are routinely neglected. Spirituality is separated from the treatment process as if it were an irrelevant topic or a subject so esoteric that it falls outside the bounds of psychotherapy. (2007, p. 7)

Bergin & Payne question the fact that an enterprise that "fosters individualism, free expression, and tolerance of dissent, would be so reluctant to address one of the most fundamental concerns of humankind—morality and spirituality" (1991, p. 201).

What is this reluctance about I wonder? What are its origins, why does spirituality seem such a "no-go area" for so many therapists? It is hardly surprising that clients may decide to leave their spirituality and faith at the door of the therapy room, fearful of their therapist's possible response or, alternatively, may deliberately decide to seek out a therapist who shares their faith and who they therefore assume will be willing to engage with this significant area of their life.

However, there is encouraging evidence of a change in attitudes to the inclusion of spirituality in psychological perspective and practice. In 2011, a new Code of Conduct was developed by the United Kingdom Board of Healthcare Chaplaincy which states:

"It is vital that spiritual services are delivered appropriately to patients and their families" (www.dhsspsni.gov.uk)—another significant indicator of the importance of meeting spiritual, as well as physical and psychological, needs.

Another example of this shift was the inauguration, in 1999, by the Royal College of Psychiatrists of a Special Interest Group (Spirituality) (SIG) and the publication in 2009 of *Spirituality and Psychiatry*, edited by Cook, Powell, and Sims in which they address a range of issues relating to spirituality and mental health in a United Kingdom context. In the same year, NHS Healthcare for Scotland published *Spiritual Care Matters* (2009), a resource for all NHS staff in Scotland, in which they summarise discussions held at the World Health Organisation in 1948 reminding us of the statement made at that meeting that "health is not just the absence of disease, it is a state of physical, psychological, social and *spiritual* well being" (p. 6, italics mine). Another indicator of this shift was the recognition of a need for the British Association for Counselling and Psychotherapy (BACP) Information Sheet "*Working with Issues of Spirituality and Faith*" (Harborne, 2008).

Benefits of integrating spirituality into therapy

Swinton, after reviewing recent literature and research, puts forward the following hypothesis:

> In opposition to post-Enlightenment ideas of the social construction of religion ... it is actually *secularisation* that is socially constructed in opposition to the natural human experience of spirituality. While people who suggest the significance of spirituality for mental health care are often accused of imposing alien values on vulnerable people, if the evidence presented thus far is correct, then *not* to address the spiritual dimensions of patients' experiences is to risk imposing false, secular values on vulnerable people. (2001, p. 3)

Therapists and mental health practitioners who have explored this question indicate the potential value of addressing clients' spiritual experience and practice. Much of what has been written in the past on this subject has come from the United States but, among others, UK psychiatrists Culliford and Eagger have turned their attention to practical considerations of integrating spirituality into mental health practice and, in answer to the question "Why assess a person's spirituality" they offer the following reasons:

1. The very nature of spirituality as a source of vitality, motivation and a healthy sense of belonging and being valued.
2. The long historical relationship between religion, medicine, and mental healthcare.
3. The patients' wishes as well as those of carers.
4. The epidemiology of spirituality/religion and mental health.
5. The influence of spirituality/religion on the attitudes and decisions of psychiatric staff. (2009, p. 17).

They go on to emphasise that, in dealing with spiritual matters with patients, it can be helpful to use ordinary rather than specifically religious language (ibid., p. 17) and suggest two types of question that may be helpful in initial enquiry:

1. What helps you most when things are difficult, when times are hard … What is really important in your life? …
2. Do you think of yourself as being either religious or spiritual? (ibid., pp. 22–23).

We can also learn much from what has already been written in a United States context by, among others, Griffith and Griffith who state that "there are times when a therapist's *most useful role* is one in which he or she helps a person to maximise the healing potential of relationships within a spiritual community" (2002, p. 191, italics mine). Richards & Bergin (1997, p. 127) suggest that spirituality should be added to Lazarus' (1976) multimodal framework. This approach advocated the exploration of the individual's BASIC ID—that is, their Behaviour (B), Affect (A), Sensation (S), Imagery (I), Cognition (C), Interpersonal relationships (D), and Drugs or biology (D)—and, if Spirituality were added, developing the model into BASIC IDS.

Griffith and Griffith (2002, Chapter Two) consider very carefully what to look for and how to recognise the presence of a spiritual element in what the client brings. However, their approach to this is not particularly different from an approach to any other material, that is, they emphasise the need to listen carefully and to pay full attention to the words that the client is using and to hold a position of "intentional uncertainty" (ibid., p. 48). They comment: "Opening conversation to talk about spirituality or religion depends less on knowing what questions to ask and more on careful listening to what people spontaneously speak about when they feel safe and respected" (ibid., p. 45) and continue by suggesting that, if spirituality is not overtly mentioned, then they might ask a direct question, for example, "Are there important beliefs that I should know about for our work together?" (ibid., p. 45).

Alternatively (and less directly) they suggest asking more existential questions as a way of introducing the subject: "From what sources do you draw strength in order to cope?" or "Where do you find peace?" (ibid., p. 46). However, they also stress that there are times when it would not be right to pursue this direction, when it would be good to ask ourselves whether this is more about our own interests/agenda rather than that of the client. They are mindful of the importance of "learning to ask questions that are carefully tailored to open dialogue, to foster reflection, or to prompt therapeutic change" (ibid, p. 48).

Pargament goes so far as to state: "Spirituality is ... another dimension of life. An extraordinary dimension, yes, but one that is a vital part of ordinary life and what it means to be human. We are more than psychological, social, and physical beings; we are also spiritual beings" (2007, p. 4). He also emphasises the necessity for trust in the client/therapist relationship:

> The therapist earns an invitation to enter the spiritual world of the client by conveying his or her deep interest in seeing life as it looks through the client's eyes and ... a willingness to be taught by the client, especially in the spiritual realm. *There is no crime to admitting a lack of knowledge—far from it. A little dose of therapeutic humility can empower clients.* (2007, p. 203, italics mine)

Pargament goes on to suggest three specific areas for more explicit examination: the place of spirituality in the client's life, the part that spirituality plays in the client's problems, and how much spirituality could be part of the solution to these problems. He offers a detailed Evaluative Framework to help the clinician to assess where the client is in terms of their spirituality, the effect this is having on their life, and what resources the client can draw on (2007, p. 222).

If we take the view that spirituality is as much a part of the self as emotional, cognitive, or physical factors, then it would be helpful to consider how this may be addressed in the initial meeting with the client, either implicitly or explicitly. It is perhaps easy for us as therapists to lose a sense of the anxiety that many clients feel when first meeting a therapist, particularly when this is at a time of crisis in their life. It is important to be mindful of the fact that their preconceptions and even previous experience of therapy may lead them to suspect that their spiritual life will be viewed with suspicion or hostility, so an attitude of gentle enquiry in order to "give permission" to express their beliefs may be necessary.

When spiritual issues are the focus of therapy

As I have described elsewhere, spiritual issues may be explicit or implicit:

1. Explicit issues of belief which are causing distress or difficulty, e.g., loss or questioning of faith.
2. Explicit issues arising from within a belief-sharing community e.g., relationships within that community.
3. Implicit issues, e.g., bereavement, relationship, sexuality, depression, seen with a specific spiritual perspective.
4. Explicit issues arising from outside a belief-sharing community e.g., family or peer pressure not to join, or to leave, the community. (Harborne, 2008, p. 1).

When we come to implicit issues of spirituality, the presenting material may not initially indicate a spiritual or religious element. For example, the purpose of therapy may appear to be to deal with bereavement or divorce but, on deeper exploration, it may subsequently become clear that there are underlying questions of faith or spirituality, such as life after death or broken wedding vows. Even if we do not share the particular beliefs of our client, we can endeavour to enter sufficiently into their frame of reference to be able to offer a therapeutic relationship in which healing can take place. If we truly believe in the autonomy of the client, that is, if we privilege the client's right to be self-governing, then we can maintain a position of respectful neutrality. As Richards & Bergin state when writing about helping clients to achieve their spiritual goals: "Regardless of their own spiritual beliefs, if therapists are willing to expand their ... sensitivity and competency into the religious and spiritual domains, we believe that they can ... often assist clients with these important goals" (1997, p. 191).

Either explicitly or implicitly, clients may bring feelings of shame and worthlessness into therapy, perhaps arising from some particular aspect of doctrine which suggests a process of sin, guilt, atonement, forgiveness, salvation. Clients, unable to move from the feelings of sin and guilt to recognition of atonement and acceptance of forgiveness and salvation, experience a double blow—not only are they sinful and guilty, but they are so sinful and guilty that they cannot even accept God's generosity and forgiveness, despite the fact that they claim to believe in the Christian message of salvation through grace.

Members of a faith community may feel abused, bullied, neglected, or exploited by the leadership, or by other members, of their community, with the result that a client's relationship with their church becomes the actual cause of their distress In such cases, therapy involves the complexities of working with issues of trauma, compounded with the added factor of working in the area of spiritual betrayal. I find it difficult to see how the abuse can effectively be addressed in therapy without simultaneously addressing the particularly profound effects of the unique context in which it has occurred.

In my own clinical work I have come across a number of clients who present with religious or faith issues where there is evidence of trauma arising from abuse. Herman describes traumatic events as follows:

> They shatter the construction of the self that is formed and sustained in relation to others. They undermine the belief systems that give meaning to human experience. They violate the victim's faith in a natural or divine order and cast the victim into a state of existential crisis ... In situations of terror, people spontaneously seek their first source of ... protection ... (they) cry for their mothers *or for God*. (1992, p. 50, italics mine)

With this in mind, I would conceptualise my clients' narrative in terms of trauma and find myself considering what a human response might be to an experience that leads us to conclude that it is God Himself, embodied in organised religion, who has abandoned us? How can this experience be integrated into our personal schemata? Trauma leads to a loss of trust in ourselves, in others, and in God.

As I have described elsewhere (Harborne, 2006. p. 51), such trauma was experienced by Polly, already elderly when she came for therapy. During World War II, as a young child, Polly had been abused by a priest, who had ensured her silence by telling her she would undoubtedly go to hell if she divulged anything to anyone. In her young mind she had linked her unspoken fear of hell with the reality of what was going on all around in her experience of the flames and catastrophe of the London blitz. Despite such symptoms of trauma as nightmares and flashbacks throughout the intervening years, she had remained faithful in her religious observance all her life, but a particularly distressing and powerful flashback, evoked by the fusty smell of vestments in a dark vestry, finally brought her to therapy. Working entirely at her pace, therapy was a slow process, but we were able to examine the effects of the abuse itself on her sense of self and also on her understanding of her relationship with God.

In working with explicitly spiritual issues and in seeking to integrate sound theory with lived experience, I find the ideas of self-psychologist Kohut (1971) very helpful. Kohut calls our intrapsychic experience of another a "selfobject" and suggests that this internalisation is essential to the development of an integrated sense of self. His proposal that in adulthood we still seek out others to meet our selfobject needs leads me to ask whether God might be described as the ultimate selfobject? Without a sufficient intrapsychic experience of God, is it possible to sustain "the cohesion, vitality or integrity of the self" (Corbett, 1996, p. 26)? If we consider that God is the ultimate selfobject, then to feel abandoned by Him must be the ultimate betrayal.

However, there may be circumstances when it is clear that a client would benefit from working with a spiritual director and, as with any referral, it is helpful if the therapist has some information about the process of finding a director in their locality.

Conclusion

As with any specific issue that clients bring to therapy, it is the task of the therapist to endeavour to enter their clients' frame of reference. While maintaining an attitude of non-judgmental enquiry, as therapists we can explore clients' material, being mindful of the danger of making assumptions and of failing to bracket our own experiences and beliefs. As in any other area of our work, the importance of being aware of factors that may influence our thinking cannot be overestimated.

If a therapist is either unwilling or unable to engage with spiritual issues with clients, then the most ethical course of action would seem to be to refer the client to someone else with competence in this area. As already indicated, I am uneasy about a therapist who is willing to "do part of the work" but who is unwilling to address anything spiritual, even when it permeates all the issues being raised in therapy. People's faith is at the core of who they are, it underpins their whole world view, their personality and how they live their life, and therefore to attempt to see it as separate would seem to be trying to split off something that is deeply embedded and integral to their whole being.

The ethical and therapeutic pitfalls that arise when a client attempts to work with two therapists simultaneously are well known, so the implications of a client taking part of their material elsewhere need to be considered carefully, particularly if this is at the suggestion or insistence of the therapist. However, while it is not uncommon for a client to see both a therapist and a spiritual director concurrently, some therapists are not happy with this situation and insist that spiritual direction is suspended for the duration of the therapy. In this situation a client can find themselves prohibited from bringing their spirituality into therapy, being told they must "take it elsewhere" and then being prevented from doing so—truly a Catch 22 situation.

Whether or not to agree to work with a client who brings explicit issues of belief is an ethical question that every therapist will need to ask themselves. If, for whatever reason, they find themselves unable to maintain a position of questioning enquiry, empathy, and unconditional positive regard, then their ability to stay in psychological contact with the client will be jeopardised. They may also consider that their ability to be authentic is also compromised if they are aware that their own personal spiritual views are diametrically opposed to those of their client.

Having considered the evidence presented by so many with experience in the fields of therapy and mental health, both as practitioners and clients, I can only conclude that there is an ethical imperative, rather than a professional option, to address our clients' spirituality. And, if we accept Swinton's (2001) view that it is secularisation rather than spirituality that is socially constructed, then as therapists we have a duty to inform and resource ourselves adequately in order to engage in this area of our clients' lives.

Finally, I am also interested in the effect that working with a client's spiritual or faith issues may have on us as therapists. If, as I believe, therapy is a process of co-creation, it is impossible that I will remain unchanged by the encounter with my clients. What are the implications for me as a therapist? I also recognise the contribution that my own spiritual practice outside the therapy room makes to what goes on inside it. As a spiritual being, I must both affect and be affected by what is going on in spiritual terms when I meet with my clients. I find this a most humbling realisation, which makes me reflect very deeply on the question of just how any of us can be considered "suitable" for this area of work—and how personally I can support myself as a therapist.

CHAPTER FOUR

Psychological issues in spiritual direction

"What is madness but nobility of the soul at odds with circumstance ..."

—Theodore Roethke 1908–1963

Introduction

Having explored the subject of the inclusion of spiritual questions in therapy in the previous chapter, we now come to the question of how to recognise and engage with psychological issues in spiritual direction. This chapter will look at the nature of the spiritual direction encounter, the desirability of initial history taking, and whether and how a risk assessment may be formulated. The whole area of working with clergy will be explored, together with the importance of a sound understanding of unconscious process. Questions about the difficulties and ambiguities that present themselves when we try to differentiate between psychosis and mysticism will be raised, and ethical and possible legal consequences identified. When and how to refer will form the final part of the chapter.

Having urged therapists to be willing to explore spiritual issues with their clients, I find myself wondering whether I hold the same attitude to spiritual directors whose directees present with psychological issues, and, if not, why not. In reality, I do see some differences in the two situations as they exist at the moment. Firstly, far fewer people enter spiritual direction in a state of crisis, or even acute personal difficulty, than is the case for therapy clients, so the inherent dangers are considerably less. There is also the question of the interval between sessions. Psychotherapy is likely to be on a weekly basis while spiritual direction may well only take place every few weeks or even months, which is a significant difference. However, it is worth noting that a particular model of spiritual direction, which follows the "Spiritual Exercises" of St Ignatius, is offered either on a daily basis for thirty days or on a weekly basis over a period of months, thus reflecting the therapeutic tradition.

The injunction "Do no harm" must surely apply to both endeavours, but the risk of lasting damage would seem to be greater when dealing with a significantly higher percentage of very distressed and vulnerable clients than is likely to be the case with spiritual directees. However, it would be dangerous to assume that no-one entering into spiritual direction is bringing serious psychological problems, so the director must be aware of this possibility and alert to possible warning signs.

The focus of spiritual direction

The focus of spiritual direction is the directee's relationship with God, which may sound very different from the sort of presenting material that might be considered "normal" in therapy. However, in practice, in order to explore this relationship effectively, it may well be relevant to pay attention to other relationships and events in the directee's life, making the content of spiritual direction not so very different from that of therapy after all. It is often difficult—even impossible—to disentangle implicit issues from the more explicit material brought to spiritual direction. If we accept the Christian belief that God is in all things, then taking the stance that anything of particular concern to a directee is outside the scope of spiritual direction would seem to be inconsistent. Additionally, it would seem to be detracting from a directee's autonomy if I, as director, steer them away from a particular topic.

History taking and risk assessment

I am aware that some directors are reluctant to make enquiries about the reason a directee has decided to seek spiritual direction at that particular moment. In my own practice, I find this a useful part of our initial conversation as it may facilitate enquiry into previous experience of therapy, and be helpful in establishing the working alliance.

Therapists have an ethical responsibility to work within their personal limits of competence and I would maintain that this is exactly the same for spiritual directors. However, my experience as supervisor suggests that directors may often be only too quick to question and devalue their own expertise and I would very much like to encourage directors to recognise their strengths and effectiveness, while still being willing to own their limitations when appropriate.

However, there may be some presenting material which needs more specific help than most spiritual directors can offer, such as depression, anxiety, addictions, and trauma, all of which are serious and even life-threatening conditions. If significant psychological conditions emerge in the course of spiritual direction, then the directee can be affirmed in their willingness to acknowledge their difficulties and can be encouraged to reflect on what other possible intervention might be considered. The very act of "normalising" these situations by talking about them can be extremely useful in providing the most appropriate help. Coming for spiritual direction may thus be the first step in a process of transformation, and we do well not to forget the centrality of the relationship between director and directee, implicit within which is the relationship between directee and God. So, while the decision to seek other help may be agreed, the directee may still find the support of the director of immense value.

Working with clergy

The difficulty of indentifying what is relevant to spiritual direction and what might better be dealt with elsewhere may be particularly relevant when working with clergy whose personal and professional lives are so interwoven that any attempt to make such a differentiation can be extremely difficult and even pointless. However, as already mentioned in Chapter Three, I am also aware that some clergy will present for spiritual direction when it is clear that weekly therapy is what is required, for example, in cases of addiction or depression. As we have seen, in some church circles therapy still carries a stigma, whereas spiritual direction is considered acceptable and appropriate for both ministers and laity. This state of affairs may encourage clergy and others, consciously or unconsciously, to seek out a director with a therapeutic background in an attempt to become "backdoor clients".

In my experience of working with clergy, it is not uncommon for them to request spiritual direction, telling stories of overwork, expressing feelings of resentment, describing misunderstandings and conflict with congregations, church superiors, or fellow clergy– all of which can lead to feelings of low self-esteem and depression. It may be, that in order to address these issues, therapy would be more appropriate, as meeting every month or six weeks (common practice in spiritual direction) will not be an effective way to address their situation. I also find that making such a suggestion may help the directee to recognise the true nature of their experience rather than falling into the temptation of "spiritualising" what is going on, perhaps by asking such questions as "What does God want me to do?" or "How can I say 'no' to the Lord's work?" If the church has unreasonable expectations of its "employees", then that is a situation that needs addressing just as much as in a secular setting. But if the client's sense of self is bound up with their identity as a priest, then therapy may help to explore the nature of this underlying belief. I am aware that, for some, this process may challenge their understanding of the theological arguments about the ontological change that ordination to priesthood confers and this, too, may need exploring as therapy progresses.

Anger and conflict in relation to church or faith settings are also common catalysts that bring people into therapy and here again the effects may seem disproportionate to the "story" being presented. This is perhaps not surprising when we consider that much teaching in such settings is against expressing (or even experiencing) anger and that the concept of forgiveness is a central part of the Christian message. It is not uncommon for Christian clients to express a sense of personal failure in coming to therapy, which may also be the view of their pastor or church leader and others in their faith community. The thinking behind such a sense of failure is often that prayer alone should be sufficient. Similarly, these clients may be particularly reluctant to take medication. These attitudes can result in clients experiencing a deep sense of failure that they are not living up to their own, their church's, and God's ideals. In such circumstances, I am reminded of what Hart says: "Medication is rarely a total answer. It is certainly not a substitute for facing one's life issues and working them through to some kind of resolution, growing through the process. Its purpose is not to put someone in a fog so they do not have to think, but only to put some kind of flooring under their emotional life so they can think clearly to work on their problems" (2002, p. 74).

Depression is as common among clergy as it is in the general population and I would suggest that this may often arise as a result of feeling like a square peg in a round hole. Many of those drawn to expressing their vocation in church ministry can be identified as introverts who find themselves in a role that is more suited to extroverts. The typical profile of dedicated clergy would indicate someone with great commitment to putting God and others before self. This combination of what may sometimes become an unrealistic sense of duty and service, together with a personality type that finds constant contact with others completely exhausting, can lead (perhaps inevitably *will* lead) to burnout and depression.

This preference, coupled with insufficient support in terms of supervision and a structural reluctance to ask for any professional help, coalesces until, sadly, the unsupported individual hits the buffers in one way or another. Much of this lack of support may arise out of the current lack of a professional human resource function in church institutions (although in some cases this is beginning to change) but clergy themselves sometimes seem to have an unrealistic expectation that their needs will be met by the institution in which they place their allegiance. This is perhaps a residual hangover from the culture and traditions prevalent before World War II, when the status vested in clergy ensured an attitude of respectful deference from their parishioners and a sense that their material needs would be provided for by others. I find that it is not unusual for clergy to demonstrate a sense of entitlement in expecting spiritual direction (and in some cases even therapy) to be free of charge just because they *are* clergy. Perhaps it can be considered a legitimate expense of their calling, but that is a matter between themselves and their "employer" rather than between themselves and their spiritual director. The cost of therapy or spiritual direction may involve financial sacrifice for many and may be considered as a sign of commitment to the process– a sacrifice that is not unique to clergy.

Unconscious process

Another factor that is acknowledged in therapy but less so in spiritual direction is that of unconscious process, such as transference, countertransference, projection, projective identification, and defence mechanisms. These are complex concepts and competent theoretical training is necessary if they are to be fully recognised and understood.

The term "transference" relates to a process of carrying over past psychological experience to a current situation or relationship in a way that is inappropriate in the present circumstances. This leads to a reaction in the present as if to events in the past in an attempt to resolve unfinished business and as a way of making sense of the current world. Countertransference is the response elicited in the therapist/director by a client/directee's unconscious transference in terms of both thoughts and feelings.

Defence mechanisms, such as denial, suppression, displacement, sublimation, and projection, protect us from being consciously aware of a thought or feeling which we cannot tolerate. The defence allows the unconscious thought or feeling to be expressed only indirectly in a disguised form. Defences may hide a variety of thoughts or feelings such as anger, fear, sadness, depression, greed, envy, competitiveness, love, passion, admiration, dependency, selfishness, grandiosity, helplessness. It seems important that spiritual directors have at least some awareness and understanding of them in order to recognise when a directee might be defending against such unwelcome feelings.

Projection can be divided into neurotic projection or complementary projection. The former is the perception that others are operating in ways we unconsciously find objectionable in ourselves and the latter is assuming that others think and feel in the same way that we do, or where we see our own traits in others—thus we see our friends as being more like us than they really are. Projective identification is experienced when I rid myself of unmanageable bits of myself and deposit them *into* (rather than *on to*) the other in an attempt to control the other. The other will then present them back to me in a modified and manageable form.

Psychosis and spirituality

There is also the complex question of differentiating between what is considered to be psychotic and what is spiritual experience. Claridge succinctly states the dilemma as follows:

> If it is the case that spiritual beliefs and experiences are phenomeno-logically similar to the psychotic's view of the world, then should we not conclude that religions are just a form of madness and the religious merely insane? Or could we not equally well decide that those diagnosed as clinically psychotic are really misunderstood visionaries, wrongly labelled and disparaged by others who fail to share their sensitivities? (2001, p. 90)

How will the spiritual director be able to identify what is psychotic and what is genuine religious experience? In extreme examples it is probably, although not inevitably, relatively straightforward to differentiate between the two, but in less florid examples this may well not be the case.

The work of Lukoff (1985) in this area is particularly helpful. West (2000, p. 81) describes Lukoff's continuum on which pure psychosis is at one polarity and pure mysticism at the other, with a number of variants of psychotic mysticism and mystical psychosis in-between. Lukoff also draws our attention to the difference between a temporary psychotic episode and long-term psychosis, and identifies eight themes that may be present that would indicate a mystical experience, albeit with psychotic features: death, rebirth, a journey, encounters with spirits, cosmic conflict, magical powers, new society, and divine union. He also proposes five criteria: ecstatic mood; new insight or knowledge; heightened sensations (e.g., auditory or visual hallucinations or other alterations from normal perception); delusions which have some mythological connection; and the absence or disruption of thought, or incoherence.

Lukoff states that "the content of an experience alone usually does not determine whether an individual is psychotic" (1985, p. 164) and draws our attention to the importance of evidence as to whether the individual is able to establish an "intersubjective reality" with others. This in itself would seem to be a most significant factor for spiritual directors to consider in evaluating whether they can work with a directee, both in terms of competence and of their ability to stay in psychological contact with the directee.

Lukoff was instrumental in the inclusion of the category "Mystical experience with Psychotic Features (V62.89)" in the American Psychiatric Association DSM-IV, (1994, p. 685), the V coding denoting that this is not a pathological categorisation but a normal response "which can be used when the focus of clinical attention is a religious or spiritual problem".

Disordered thinking and a high level of social anxiety may also alert a spiritual director to the possibility of psychosis. Most thought processes have some apparent element of sequential logic, whereas in psychosis, thinking may be fragmented, with a loss of connection between ideas, sometimes described as being "derailed".

Religious delusions

So how may we recognise the presence of religious delusion? What are the symptoms? Sims (1992), cited in Clarke, proposes the following criteria for religious delusion:

> Both the observed behaviour and the subjective experience conform with psychiatric symptoms. The patient's self-description of the experience is recognisable as having the form of a delusion. There are other recognisable symptoms of mental illness in other areas of the individual's life; such as other delusions, hallucinations, mood or thought disorders. The lifestyle, behaviour and direction of the personal goals of the individual after the event or after the religious experience are consistent with the natural history of mental disorder rather than with a personally enriching life experience. (2001, p. 224)

Cultural factors must also be taken into account in considering what is delusional and what isn't. For a psychiatric diagnosis of delusion, the convictions must also be inconsistent with the person's cultural, educational, or religious background. Clearly, many mainstream Christian beliefs are considered delusional in a general sense by atheists, as they are firmly held yet cannot be proved empirically, but as long as they are in keeping with the generally accepted tenets of Christian teaching then they would not be considered as evidence of delusional thinking. Mitchell and Roberts remind us that

> current psychiatric convention is that beliefs shared by people with a similar religious or cultural background are not delusions, although they may be accompanied by the same phenomenological characteristics as delusion … Delusion is the cardinal symptom of insanity; the great majority of religious believers with their creeds and congregations are recognisably different from people with psychotic illness who are alone with their idiosyncratic and isolating beliefs. The mad and the religious may share some properties in both the content and the process by which they hold their beliefs but that does not make them the same. (2009, p. 45)

The strength of conviction with which a belief is held, rather than the belief itself, can also be an indicator of delusional thinking, as is the rejection of evidence to support alternative explanations.

While some therapists would no doubt disagree with me, when considering what is delusional, I would certainly also take into account the negative or positive effect on the directee. For example, if the effect of the directee's subjective experience is towards harming self or others then I would consider it more than likely to be delusional, but if the effect is to increase self-agency and encourage the directee into taking some positive step towards personal or spiritual growth, then I would be less likely to consider it delusional.

When, where, and how to refer

Recognising the imperative of working within our limits of competence—either as therapists or spiritual directors—the question arises of when it may be appropriate to refer a client/directee elsewhere in order that they may be offered an appropriate level of intervention and support. It is therefore vital that directors are aware of their own limitations.

In some circumstances it may be evident from the outset that referral to specialist services is appropriate, for example, where it is clear that there are addiction, bereavement, or mental health problems.

In order to ascertain whether or not spiritual direction with any particular director is possible or appropriate an initial exploratory meeting therefore seems essential. Some directors are reluctant to talk in terms of a "contract", and even seem to shy away from acknowledging any form of agreement, but it seems only fair to the prospective directee to check our mutual understanding of the nature and purpose of spiritual direction and to clarify the practical details involved. The question of such a "contract" is further addressed in Chapter Six.

In the event that, after such an initial session, it seems that spiritual direction is not appropriate, it is helpful if the director can suggest agencies offering specific services, for example, a counselling agency, Samaritans, Alcoholics Anonymous, or Cruse. It would therefore seem good practice for spiritual directors to become well informed about local and national resources to which they can refer when necessary.

In my experience, it is not nearly as common for spiritual directors to check out possible contraindications to engaging with a new directee as would be the case with therapists. Whereas in most settings and circumstances therapists will ask themselves questions about their levels of competence and expertise to work with a particular client, the likelihood of being able to establish an effective working alliance, and the probability of a positive outcome, it seems that spiritual directors are less likely to examine these questions and consider whether they are the best person for the directee. If they are working in isolation (as is often the case) they may not feel able to suggest an alternative director and this may discourage them from making a decision not to pursue the relationship.

There are also areas where specific expertise may need to be sought, for example, in the case of mental health issues, addiction, and trauma. This does not mean that spiritual direction cannot continue, and it may be both important and relevant to reflect on whether and when therapy and spiritual direction can co-exist. As mentioned in the previous chapter, some therapists and directors are unhappy—and sometimes unwilling—to see someone who is engaged in the other activity, thus forcing the client/directee to make a choice, possibly at a time when they are feeling particularly distressed and confused. This situation also seems to reinforce the split between therapy and direction, and it could be argued that, if therapists were more spiritually informed, they would be able to contemplate working alongside a spiritual director in the overall interests of the client. Likewise, if directors were more psychologically educated they would have greater insight into the benefits for their directee of being able to integrate spiritual aspects of their life with other dimensions.

While there may well be some circumstances where either therapy or spiritual direction on its own may be the appropriate intervention, I would prefer not to see this as an either/or situation. Many clients who are already engaged in spiritual direction may also benefit from concurrent therapy. Ideally I would hope that many more spiritual directors will train as therapists and vice versa so that total integration will be the result, but I suspect we are a long way from achieving this aim.

Conclusion

To be a competent practitioner is no less imperative for a spiritual director than for a psychotherapist—in fact it could be argued that there is an even greater expectation of the highest possible standards of practice when dealing with what we call the human soul. A belief in the presence and power of the Holy Spirit will not save us from our own ignorance, blindness, and deafness, and many spiritual directors are not aware of, or well informed about, the possibility of unconscious processes and the potential psychological dynamics in the director/directee relationship. However, ignorance cannot be a justification for inferior practice.

CHAPTER FIVE

Depression or Dark Night of the Soul?

"Depression is a label and a syndrome, while a dark night is a meaningful event."

—Thomas Moore (2004)

Purpose of the chapter

In this chapter I will attempt to define what is meant by the terms "Dark Night of the Soul" (DNS) and "depression", and to identify indicators that may help us to recognise the two conditions. I hope this will help therapists to work more effectively with the spiritual elements of their clients' experience, while enabling spiritual directors to recognise indicators of depression in order to make a competent risk assessment. I raise questions about how we can differentiate between depression and DNS—are they in fact manifestations of the same inner experience, are they two quite separate experiences, or can they be said to co-exist? And, whatever the answers to these questions, how can we address them in both therapy and spiritual direction? Nelson's view that "The dark night is really a normal process, whereas most people consider depression to be an abnormal condition" (2009, p. 378) will be considered.

This is a complex subject and I am not suggesting that it is always possible to make a clear-cut differentiation between a DNS and clinical depression. I am aware of the dangers of trying to construct definitive criteria and models of treatment and I recognise that a desire for such clarity may well arise out of discomfort at staying with uncertainty, ambivalence, and not-knowing. However, it is my hope that, working together to co-create understanding and meaning, therapist and client, director and directee, may be able to identify signs that will help in considering what might be possible—never forgetting the primacy of the individual's own understanding of what is going on for them—through phenomenological observation and attuned enquiry.

What do we mean by "The Dark Night of the Soul"?

Traditionally, the term is often associated with the writings of the Spanish mystic St John of the Cross (1542–1591), and much of what has been written offers us literary criticism rather than psychological or spiritual insight. St John's poetry, together with his own commentary, beautifully and movingly reflects his own experience. Schrock says: "The dark night is a metaphor for one of the ways God shapes us more fully into the image of Christ" (2009, p. 17) and Matthew, himself a Carmelite, states that "God's work of change John has called 'night'" (1995, p. 153).

In their writings, both St John of the Cross and St Teresa of Avila use the word "dark" in the sense of "obscure". As a psychiatrist and spiritual director, May states:

> In speaking of *la noche oscura*, the dark night of the soul, John is addressing something mysterious and unknown, but by no means sinister or evil. It is instead profoundly sacred and precious beyond all imagining ... It is the secret way in which God not only liberates us from our attachments and idolatries, but also brings us to the realization of our true nature. The night is the means by which we find our heart's desire, our freedom for love. (2005, p. 67)

This does not mean that it is an easy process; May also suggests that the darkness is so constant that "I sometimes say, 'If you're certain you're going through a dark night of the soul you probably aren't!'" (2005, p. 71). In a dark night experience, nothing can be said to be certain. And yet John says that God darkens our awareness in order to keep us safe: "Night more kindly than the dawn" (Van de Weyer, 1995, Stanza 5,

p. 4). Matthew (1995, p. 53) suggests that God's work of change is what John is referring to in the word "night". St John stresses that it is God who leads us into the dark night of the senses in order that we can be purified, drawing a parallel between this process and weaning an infant and encouraging the child to eat solid food.

St John differentiates further in describing both nights as either active or passive; in active dark nights, we engage consciously with the process (e.g., spiritual practices, self-discipline) while in passive dark nights we admit our inability to retain control and let go of our previously held convictions and expectations, leaving us better able to accept God's will. This change of outlook may feel profoundly disturbing—or sometimes profoundly liberating—resulting in an awareness of positive feelings such as joy at release from restricting attachments, increased self-knowledge, reverence for God, humility, and a deeper love of neighbour.

In *The Dark Night of the Soul* John writes of two stages of darkness. The first of these is the Dark Night of the Senses, which he considers to be a fairly common experience and which he describes as "bitter and terrible" and which he sees as evidence of God leading us from immature and limited understanding towards more mature spiritual insights. He then suggests that the second stage, which he calls the Dark Night of the Spirit, is much rarer and may overlap with the Dark Night of the Senses. The Dark Night of the Senses focuses on the five senses whereas, in writing of the Dark Night of the Spirit, John does not give us a clear description of the difference, just that the focus is on our inner, spiritual experience rather than our outer sensory experience. Schrock, in writing of Dark Night of the Spirit, says: "It is a far more intense experience of inner suffering than the night of sense" (2009, p. 18), and does not differentiate between the Night of the Senses and the Night of the Spirit, noting that the latter may be experienced as a more intense version of the former and that they may in fact occur in reverse order.

However, it is worth noting that, while St John of the Cross expresses very profoundly the effect of his own dark night, he does not offer us a definitive description, and the experience of questioning one's beliefs, feeling separated from God, or even having a sense of losing one's faith completely, is a theme that has been recorded throughout history. For example, the psalms are full of examples of what could now be identified as both DNS and depression (Psalms 34:18; 40:1–3; 61:1–2; 69; 88) and the writings in the Old Testament books of Lamentations and Job also evidence these experiences. So, while acknowledging the influence that the ideas of St John of the Cross have had on our understanding of dark night experiences, I would not want to limit the content of this chapter to the critical examination of the text of his writings.

Nelson describes the Dark Night of the Spirit as follows:

> It is a painful experience involving feelings of desolation … this darkness is actually God at work in a very intimate way, with a kind of pain resulting from the nearness and purity of God working to perfect us beyond our normal capacities … as the experience progresses, we have increasing periods with a sense of freedom, abundance, peace, and in intimate relationship with God. (2009, p. 378)

Spiritual directees will not be comparing themselves with St John of the Cross; they will be talking about their own personal experience of powerful and significant change in the nature of their faith—a change that is causing distress and confusion—and their attempt to make some meaning of this experience. Everyone's individual journey is unique, and perhaps it is only by living through such an experience, or by being alongside someone else who is having such an experience, that we will be able to make any sort of sense of what is going on. In therapeutic terms this could be linked with the experience of attunement and working at relational depth, transference and countertransference, the conscious and unconscious sharing of another's experience at a deep and wordless level.

My understanding of the concepts of the DNS and of depression originates in my personal experience and that of clients and directees, but, as I have highlighted above, I am very conscious that no two people's description will ever be identical, and I am therefore particularly mindful of the dangers of making assumptions about someone else's experience. While there may be identifying symptoms of depression, as outlined in the Diagnostic and Statistical Manual IV-TR, and there may be signs and characteristics that could be said to indicate DNS, I am reminded of the maxim that "the map is not the territory". Indeed, the very fact of having experienced something ourselves may have the apparently paradoxical effect of preventing us from entering into a client's or a directee's frame of reference with an open mind, free from assumptions.

A dark night experience is perhaps mainly about letting go of our attachments in order that our relationship with God can develop in new and liberating ways. As May says: "All major spiritual traditions have long understood that attachment binds the energy of the human spirit to something other than love ... We want to be free, compassionate, and happy, but in the face of our attachments we are clinging, grasping, and fearfully self-absorbed" (2005, pp. 60–61).

Letting go of such attachments is a risky and terrifying business with uncertain—yet transforming—consequences. While we may sometimes use the term "Dark Night of the Soul" quite loosely to indicate a difficult transition or a taxing inner struggle, we may also be referring to a particular experience of change in the nature and quality of our faith.

In identifying characteristics that would seem to indicate a dark night experience, May draws our attention to the three essential signs that John of the Cross identifies in *Dark Night of the Soul Bk 1 Ch 9* (Van de Weyer, 1995, pp. 36–39) and these are factors that we can explore with directees:

1. Dryness and impotence in prayer and life—what was previously enriching, no longer satisfies.
2. Lack of desire for the old ways of prayer and living.
3. A simple desire to love God. (2005, pp. 138–142).

May suggests that we are hard-wired for attachment to God and that it is our reluctance that keeps this out of awareness. Awareness, when it comes, can be pleasurable (realisation of what we want) or painful (realisation of the emptiness of former attachments). In his exploration of the Dark Night of the Senses, May recognises the difficulty of maintaining spiritual practice and of answering the question that may emerge: "Do I believe in anything any more? Do I care?"

Matthew states that not all spiritual suffering is dark night and lists the necessary hallmarks of a dark night experience as:

- An inflow of God
- Darkness, that is, the suffering, with the accent on bewildering suffering
- A creative response—faith, acceptance. (1995, p. 72)

However, the lasting results of a DNS can be transformative. Schrock suggests the following may be the outcome:

- Faith deepens in the face of the suffering
- Our relationship with God changes and becomes an intimate friendship
- Our life in the world takes on the character of a countercultural mission. (2009, p. 170)

What is depression?

Perhaps one of the most vivid descriptions of the serious and potentially life-threatening effects of clinical depression can be found in the opening words of *Darkness Visible* by William Styron: "In Paris on a chilly evening in October of 1985 I first became fully aware that the struggle with the disorder in my mind … might have a fatal outcome" (1992, p. 1). It is also interesting to note that Styron prefaces this account of his experience by quoting from Job: "For the thing which I greatly feared is come upon me, and that which I was afraid of is come unto me. I was not in safety, neither had I rest, neither was I quiet; yet trouble came". (Job 3:25–26)

From a clinical point of view, the criteria for a major depressive disorder are listed in American Psychiatric Association DSM-IV-TR, which I summarise as follows:

The presence of 5 or more of the following symptoms which are experienced nearly every day during a 2 week period and one of which at least is either depressed mood or loss of interest or pleasure:

1. Depressed mood most of the day.
2. Markedly diminished interest or pleasure in almost all activities most of the day.
3. Significant weight loss or weight gain, or decrease or increase in appetite.
4. Insomnia or hypersomnia.
5. Psychomotor agitation or retardation, observable by others.
6. Fatigue or loss of energy.
7. Feeling of worthlessness or excessive or inappropriate guilt.
8. Diminished ability to think or concentrate, or indecisiveness.
9. Recurrent thoughts of death or suicidal ideation or planning suicide. (1994, p. 327)

While it is important to remember that most therapists and spiritual directors are not medically trained, it is not unreasonable for them to be mindful of the above symptoms, the presence of which may indicate clinical depression. Clients in general, and those with a religious background in particular, may often be very reluctant to take anti-depressant medication and are therefore determined to avoid the doctor's surgery. This reluctance may need to be honoured, but nevertheless I consider it my ethical duty, either as therapist or spiritual director, to raise the possibility that they might talk with their general practitioner about their symptoms. I consider it unethical to ignore the evidence of possible mental health issues and would also want to explore with a client who acknowledges such symptoms what any reluctance to ask for medical help might be about.

It could well be that the very cause of this reluctance may also lie at the root of the depression, that is, a fear of appearing inadequate, supported by a core belief that their individual worth has to be earned, together with low self-esteem and an overriding conviction that accepting medical help would indicate a personal weakness. So the very condition that the client is experiencing works against taking the steps that could prove most helpful. This is why I see detailed enquiry by therapist or spiritual director about the client's current inner experience as an essential and ethical intervention in order to make a competent risk assessment.

My personal experience

My thinking about depression and DNS is rooted in my own experience. What I would now consider to be my first DNS experience occurred in my early thirties. Having been brought up as a practising Anglican, I found myself married with two young children, and seriously questioning my Christian beliefs for the first time. I can remember quite clearly acknowledging to myself that, if my faith was without foundation, then my whole life was built on a misconception. Not only can I still remember my thought process, but I can also remember the enormous wave of terror that followed—nothing was certain for me any more. The implications of this were almost overwhelming and, at that moment, I felt overcome with fear. With hindsight, my first DNS was just beginning. For nearly five years I underwent a time of huge transformation, of deconstruction, and, eventually, reconstruction—a process that is never complete, never finished. That may all sound very tidy but in fact it was an extremely messy and destabilising experience.

Some twenty years later, as a result of a variety of totally unforeseen and somewhat bizarre circumstances, I found myself "at odds" with my church community again. So I entered into what I would now call the Dark Night of the Spirit. This was, however, a very different interior experience. Again, my whole life was being turned upside down; I was completely re-evaluating my beliefs; what had previously nourished my spiritual life no longer did; I actually wondered whether I was losing my sense of reality and going mad; I was totally at sea; and yet I have never—before or since—felt as close to God as I did during this period, which was at its most acute for about two years, and elements of which lingered for several years after that.

Survival became the imperative. I knew I could not make any major decisions, in fact making even a minor decision became risky. My immediate family and a few friends stuck with me and I owe them the most enormous debt of gratitude as my distress—or what I can only call anguish—spilled out into all my relationships. I sought both therapy and formal spiritual direction and, in so doing, changed the course of my life. Yet again, God allowed me the freedom to make my own choices, while never abandoning me to the worst effects of my mistakes. I thought I had hit rock bottom on several occasions, only to find that there was another cavernous drop yet to be navigated, and another, and another!

When I reflect on my own experience of DNS, the most powerful memory is that of uncertainty about everything—except for the fact that there could be no going back. At all levels I was aware that life could and would never be the same. To revert to my previously held beliefs and behaviours could never be an authentic option. I was changing, *being changed*, at a fundamental level.

The two personal experiences that I have described above differed from each other—and do not exactly match either May or Schrock's descriptions. In the first of these periods, I lost any sense of God's presence but was aware of an overwhelming desire and yearning to recapture, renew, recreate what had been so important in my life in the past, while paradoxically also recognising the truth that there could be no going back. The second period felt very different: while I did sometimes miss a certain sense of fellowship that being part of a church community had provided, this was far outweighed by a deep and life-giving sense of freedom and liberation. However, when May writes of the difficulty of maintaining spiritual practice and of the emerging question "Do I believe in anything any more? Do I care?", it is this "Do I care?" element that is particularly powerful. For me, this wasn't a question about indifference but rather a liberation from previously held beliefs; I had permission to think differently. And implicit in this was a challenge to integrate the past with the present and the future, rather than completely jettison old ideas in favour of new beliefs: the new emerged out of the old. But, again, one thing was completely clear to me, there was absolutely no question about it—there could be no going back.

So, from my own experience, how would I distinguish DNS experience from clinical depression—if, indeed, I would make such a distinction? In both instances I would recognise the presence of some elements of depression, although this was much more marked in the second case, when I did actually feel depressed, and suffered significant weight loss and insomnia. However, with hindsight, I would now suggest that the feelings of depression actually arose out of the dark night experience and perhaps it was not unreasonable to feel depressed when the whole belief system that had previously underpinned my life had been swept away. There was a real sense of looking into a void, with all the resulting terror that this evoked, reminiscent of the "demons" that the Desert Fathers faced in their isolation and solitude.

I would therefore suggest that depression and DNS may well co-exist and it is worth noting that James (1985) was always more drawn to religion at times when he most suffered from bouts of depression. Perhaps there can be a strong element of cause and effect—struggles with faith providing the cause, with depression the outcome. Thus depression can be seen as a "normal" response in a period of significant spiritual change and growth.

Similarly, this would seem to be reflected in the words of Merton: "The secret of my identity is hidden in the love and mercy of God … If I find Him I will find myself … I cannot hope to find myself anywhere except in Him" (1961, p. 35). This demonstrates Merton's belief in the link between a strong sense of self and the relationship with God so that, when experiencing the absence of a felt sense of God's presence, the sense of self will also seem to be annihilated. Thus the effects of DNS and depression may seem to merge.

Equally, it is perhaps not unreasonable to suspect that people experiencing clinical depression may also very easily find that their faith changes and may even be undermined. Might they not be asking themselves—and perhaps others—"Where is God for me when I feel so wretched and awful and when life seems to have no meaning whatsoever and I can take no pleasure in anything?"

Similarities and differences: how can we differentiate?

Moore states: "Depression is a psychological sickness, a dark night is a spiritual trial" (2004, p. xiv). He continues: "I see a dark night of the soul as a period of transformation" (ibid., p. xvi). It therefore seems that, while a dark night may have elements of depression, it is nevertheless a transforming experience, whereas depression itself requires healing. However, the transformational nature of DNS may not be at all evident at the time: it is often only with hindsight that these positive aspects can be clearly seen.

From his experience as a psychiatrist and as a spiritual director, May identifies the following indicators that differentiate between a dark night experience and depression and which I summarise as follows:

1. Dark night experiences are not usually associated with loss of effectiveness in life or work as is often the case with depression.
2. Sense of humour usually retained in dark night of the soul.
3. Compassion for others retained or increased rather than the self-absorption that is often present in depression.
4. In spite of everything, the individual can acknowledge an underlying sense of rightness about the experience.
5. Seldom does the person seem to be begging "Get me out of this".
6. The person working with someone experiencing a dark night does not generally find themselves feeling frustrated, resentful or annoyed as may be the case when working with depression. (1992, p. 109)

Culligan (in Egan) distinguishes between the two conditions as follows:

> Although loss is common to both, this loss is manifested differently in each case. In the dryness of the dark night of sense, for example, there is a loss of pleasure "in the things of God" … but there is not the dysphoric mood, the psychomotor retardation, the loss of energy or pleasure in hobbies and enjoyable activities, including sex, that

one typically sees in clinical depression. And, while those in the dryness of the dark night of sense are unable to apply their minds and imagination to discursive meditation, they have little difficulty in concentrating and making decisions in daily life. (2003, p. 130)

As we have seen, May (1992, p. 109) suggests that a dark night experience is not usually associated with loss of effectiveness in life or work, whereas this is often an outcome of depression. Despite the dark night experience, a sense of humour is usually retained along with a sense of a compassion for others, while during a period of depression, individuals will often experience increased self-absorption and subsequent isolation which is, I would suggest, the result of the survival imperative. When struggling for this survival, all energy is invested in maintaining a sense of self, leaving nothing spare for anything else.

However, it is this very absorption with self, leading perhaps to withdrawal from others, that can cause the burden of isolation to be added to the depression experience. We can find ourselves in the paradoxical and contradictory situation of withdrawing from relationship with others and then blaming those very same people for negligence, accusing them of a lack of interest in us and care for us. And the paranoia that so often accompanies the anxiety that is an undertow in times of depression, convinces us that our accusations of negligence are well founded and legitimate. In this state, our unapproachability renders us our own worst enemy; yet we may long to be approached, to be nurtured, and to belong to a caring community, despite the apparent evidence to the contrary.

It is in exactly these circumstances that the relationship with a spiritual director or a therapist can become an absolute lifeline. Here is one person who is willing to maintain an emotional connection with me, with whom I can be completely open and authentic and who, because of their training and their role, will be psychologically robust enough not to be damaged through their contact with me and with all that I bring into our sessions. There is also the added dimension that, certainly in the case of a spiritual director, and sometimes in the case of a therapist, our engagement will be supported by prayer.

It seems to me that, if there is an element common to all—or almost all—experiences of DNS, then that element is the demand, the necessity, the imperative, to let go of the attachments that have claimed our attention and our energy. Precisely because we hold these attachments so dear, it is particularly difficult and painful for us to surrender them. This is the task of the dark night, and the process is not complete until the letting go has been absolute—it is a stripping bare, not a remodelling. In this process there are no certainties about what I will look like at the end; it isn't a case of changing my spiritual clothes, it is a case of being willing to relinquish everything with absolutely no certainty or guarantee that something else will fill the void. Above all we cannot know the outcome. This is a wilderness with no boundaries—we cannot be sure that there will be an oasis if we keep travelling. A dark night experience moves relentlessly on, without our conscious consent; it happens whether we like it or not.

O'Collins (1995, p. 67) writes of what he calls "Counterfeit Destinations", that is, the temptation to be sidetracked or to cut short this tumultuous journey by settling for something—anything in fact—that may look as though it might give relief from the psychological, emotional, and spiritual agony. Such a "safe harbour" may have value in that it offers respite but, unless the journey has genuinely been embraced and completed, then respite is all that will be gained. In the long run, such staging points must be recognised for what they are, otherwise they will deteriorate into "Counterfeit Destinations". And how will we know the difference between the real and the counterfeit?

Jamieson describes what he calls "waystations" as follows: "the waystation provides a place or a space for an individual to explore and find meaning, develop identity and connect with the Spirit of God. The waystation calls an individual to reconsider their life at all levels by their encounter with an alternative reality" (2007, p. 102). Identifying such spaces may be central to the way we work with those immersed in a dark night experience.

It may be particularly difficult to differentiate between depression and DNS in cases where emotional distress is the result of conflict, harassment, or neglect from within a church community. When this distress is rooted in the very place where people express their faith, then it is sometimes very easy to assume that they are suffering from a dark night experience, whereas in fact their faith in God may be secure while their faith in the institutional church may be very shaken. For some people, the two are so conflated that, for them, it is extremely difficult to separate them, and skilful spiritual direction will be needed if they are to navigate their way through these difficulties satisfactorily. This may be particularly challenging for clergy spiritual directors (*or* directees) who will need to examine their views about belonging to a church community very carefully and honestly and with an awareness of any personal agenda that may be present.

What can we offer?

While much has been written in a UK context about strategies for working with depression, the subject of a DNS experience has been little addressed. However, May, referring to the commentary on Stanza III of *Living Flame of Love* (Van de Weyer, 1995), points out that "it is clear that Teresa and John felt the most prevalent error of spiritual directors was trying to do too much, meddling with the precious work of God in a soul" (2005, p. 169). There are dangers for both therapists and spiritual directors, who desperately want to alleviate or "fix" the suffering that arises from experiences of depression or dark night of the soul. St Teresa of Avila recognised this danger and cautioned against paying too much attention to the presenting problem rather than focusing on the process.

Schrock identifies some possible responses to the dark night that he suggests are unlikely to be helpful, all of which in one way or another would seem to be an attempt to deny the intensity and significance of this experience, which I summarise below:

- Attempting to go back to the way things were
- Trying harder
- Snapping out of it
- Refusing to accept the reality of the Night
- Giving up and walking away from God. (2009, pp. 98–102)

He does, however, give some ideas of responses that he suggests may be helpful which, again, I summarise as follows:

- Pursue God with our heart's desire
- Seek silence and solitude
- Stay connected to other Christians
- Develop skills to navigate at night, that is, allow our spirituality to develop in new ways
- Develop a contemplative prayer practice
- Find a spiritual director. (2009, pp. 98–102)

In the case of depression, medical intervention and/or therapy may be the most effective way forward and, if this is the case, spiritual directors should be aware of the limits of their competence. They may invite directees to consider the possibility of self-referring elsewhere and be willing to explore the nature of any reluctance to do so. At this point it may also be worth raising the question of the director's own personal attitudes to mental health issues and diagnosis; if we ourselves wouldn't be willing to seek medical intervention, or would be reluctant to consider the possibility of medication, it may be difficult for us authentically to engage with our directees in this area. Yet depression can be a life-threatening condition, needing specialist and possibly long-term treatment and, in such circumstances, spiritual directors would do well to remember the advice given in Ecclesiasticus 8:13 that "There are times when good health depends on doctors".

I constantly come back to the fact that good basic listening skills should not be overlooked when working with either clients or directees. In maintaining Rogers' core conditions of empathy, unconditional positive regard, and congruence, both therapist and director are offering those with whom they work the foundations for a healing relationship.

When facing instances of depression, it will be our willingness as spiritual directors to stay with our directees' individual experience and our ability to contain their feelings, however negative, hopeless, and despairing, that will be required and, in some cases, will be tested to the limit. In these circumstances, spiritual directors would benefit from being trained in how to address the possibility of suicide. It may seem natural to shy away from this particularly difficult subject, yet it is clear that, rather than prompting someone into taking drastic action that they would not otherwise have thought of, openly acknowledging suicidal ideation can bring feelings of enormous relief.

While there are some therapists who may hold the view that therapy and spiritual direction cannot take place concurrently, there are those who do not see them as mutually exclusive. In the case of medical or therapeutic intervention, it may well be that the directee will find the support offered by spiritual direction to be immensely valuable and beneficial to their treatment, so the spiritual director, far from being redundant or an impediment at this time, may be very much part of an integrated and holistic healing process. May (1992, p. 193) puts the case that establishing mutual links between professionals in the psychological and spiritual worlds will be very beneficial to all involved and Dein

(2004, p. 287), himself a psychiatrist, while acknowledging that many of his colleagues see religion as primitive, guilt-inducing, and irrational, makes a plea for closer collaboration between psychiatric and religious professionals and for better training in, and openness to, each other's disciplines. Perhaps the differentiation between DNS and clinical depression is one of the key areas where mutual understanding and collaboration may be most fruitful.

Conversely, a therapist working with a client suffering from depression, may recognise significant spiritual issues that may be impeding positive progress and which could more appropriately be dealt with in spiritual direction. In such a case the interests of the client, and an ethical way forward, would seem to include addressing the possibility of enlisting the support of a spiritual director, again in the pursuit of a holistic model of treatment.

When considering how (or even whether) therapists can work with a DNS, or, conversely, spiritual directors with depression, it is apparent that there is room for improvement in both initial and on-going training. In the interests of the safety of individuals in both client groups, it would seem essential that, in future, spiritual direction training courses address the issue of depression, while therapy trainings should include paying attention to spiritual issues such as that of dark night of the soul. Clients should be able to expect a minimum level of understanding and competence in those in whom they are putting their trust. The question of how this might be addressed in training courses is considered in Chapter Nine.

In both situations it is important that practitioners pay attention to what goes on for them personally in the sessions and what feelings they experience in response to their clients. Indeed, Culligan (in Egan) goes so far as to state:

> I can usually tell whether persons are depressed or in the dark night by attending closely to my own interior reactions as these persons describe their inner experience. As a disorder of mood or affect, depression communicates across personal relationships ... After listening to depressed persons describe their suffering, I myself begin to feel helpless and hopeless, as though the dejected mood of persons with depression is contagious. (2003, p. 131)

By noting these responses, both therapists and directors can reflect on what might be going on at an unconscious level which can then inform their thinking about the work in progress and the advisability of increasing supervision and personal support. The importance of identifying this felt experience and, subsequently, being mindful of its implications cannot be too strongly emphasised, as has been addressed by Rothschild (2000 and 2006). By paying attention to transferential issues and unconscious process, the encounter between therapist and client, director and directee, may develop at a deeper level.

And, above all, we would be wise to remember that clients/directees are the experts on themselves and that, in the experience of being truly met in the encounter with therapist/director, they will be able to access their own inner resources and thus effect change and healing. Both depression and DNS demand an ability and willingness to stay with the client/directee's experience without being drawn into an understandable desire "to fix" or to short-cut the process. In both cases, we are treading on holy ground and need to be sensitive to the mystery of the needs of the other, rather than imposing our own understanding of what is going on for them.

Conclusion

Authors such as Culligan (in Egan, 2003), May (1992, 2005), Moore (2004), and Schrock (2009) identify factors that they suggest show a differentiation between depression and dark night of the soul. However, while recognising and respecting their wisdom and expertise, together with the authenticity of their reflections on personal experience, I am beginning to question just how important such a differentiation may, or may not, be in practice. I am not suggesting that these two conditions are identical but, two people may each have a diagnosis of depression—in which there may be common factors—but their personal experience of the condition may still be very different, with quite distinctive features; nevertheless, they would both admit to suffering from depression. While the causes may be different, could it be that what we label a DNS experience is in fact a very particular manifestation of depression?

I am also aware of the dangers implicit in paying too much attention to any diagnosis and, that by so doing, we must face the possibility of "missing" what the individual is actually telling us. It is possible that the importance that we attribute to the label given may come from our own desire for confirmation of the role that we are taking; in other words, are we meeting the person as their spiritual director or as their therapist? I suggest that it is our anxiety to be clear about our agenda that promotes this desire, arising out of our reluctance to stay with uncertainty and ambiguity.

I am very aware that, when listening to the stories of individuals, regardless of whether they see themselves as therapy clients or spiritual directees, I am being privileged to hear something of their deepest and most painful experience. As a result it seems increasingly unhelpful to try to differentiate between what might be labelled "Dark Night of the Soul" or, alternatively, "depression". I need to pay attention to their phenomenological experience and make myself fully available to meet them at relational depth. Is there a danger that, in trying to make a clear differentiation, the spirituality of our clients is being pathologized in psychotherapy or privileged in spiritual direction rather than being integrated in both? Why do we even try to make this distinction, rather than just meeting the other with compassion and a genuine desire for their healing?

Perhaps the only imperative is that, whatever context we find ourselves in, we are competent both to make an accurate risk assessment and willing to acknowledge our own limitations when necessary. Perhaps the question of identifying differentiation between DNS and clinical depression is an area where mutual understanding and collaboration may have the potential to be particularly fruitful.

CHAPTER SIX

Ethical and boundary issues

"Profession: (1) vow made on entering religious order;
(2) vocation or calling ... that calls for advanced learning."

—Concise Oxford Dictionary

Introduction

What do we mean by "Ethical Practice"? In the course of my work as psychotherapist and as spiritual director, I often ask myself this same question—and I find that the answer may be different depending on context. It is perhaps this area where differences become more apparent, and which will be examined in this chapter.

The use of the term "charism of spiritual direction" will be explained, together with attitudes that arise from this understanding. Ethical and boundary issues such as contracting, confidentiality, dual relationships, self-disclosure, supervision, keeping notes and records, recognising limits of competence, continuing professional development, payment, and insurance will be addressed. The lack of any code of ethics for spiritual directors in the United Kingdom is acknowledged, and the process of ethical decision-making discussed. The inclusion of prayer in sessions will be mentioned, although this will be explored in greater depth in Chapter Eight.

Some spiritual directors express a fear of what they call "over-professionalization", which often seems to be prevalent when considering ethical issues, and I hope that this chapter may help to dispel some of these fears in the interests of offering all directees a safe experience that meets their individual needs.

The charism of spiritual direction and the profession of psychotherapy

A particular concern expressed by some spiritual directors and other religious leaders is that spiritual direction may lose something of its essential nature through the introduction of conventions that are widely accepted as contributing to ethical practice in the field of psychotherapy. The Christian understanding is that charisms, or spiritual gifts, are those special abilities which are given by the Holy Spirit in order to enable individuals to offer supernatural talents in the service of God (for example, prophecy, miraculous powers, speaking in tongues as specified in 1 Corinthians 12:1–11). Many spiritual directors hold the view that they have been granted a special charism, although I would seriously question how, or whether, anyone can truly discern this about themselves. I suspect that it may often be just those people who most fervently believe that they are blessed with particular gifts who are least likely to be able to demonstrate the fruits of them in practice.

The discernment process can be an ongoing struggle, evoking tension between a willingness to surrender our own convictions, to put our perceived vocation of spiritual director to the test, and a willingness to embrace that vocation in the service of God. It would therefore seem reasonable to suggest that any charism wholly and freely given by the Holy Spirit and wholly and freely accepted by the recipient still requires reflection about its potential use. This reflection would almost certainly result in a desire and commitment to deepen understanding of this God-given gift in order fully to develop its use in God's service. As with other charisms—for example, the charisms of preaching, teaching, and healing—this would inevitably lead practitioners to engage in serious study, together with supervised practice, in order to test their calling, extend their knowledge and expertise, and make themselves accountable to others.

It is therefore important to explore the possible consequences of resistance to taking what might be considered to be a more "professional" approach (in terms of training, structure, and accountability) to the ministry of spiritual direction. In other fields, a lack of consistent and agreed standards of practice is seen as undesirable, unethical, and potentially dangerous. It is unacceptable for teachers and medical practitioners to be unqualified, uninsured, and unaccountable, and yet teaching and healing are amongst the named charisms in 1 Corinthians 12.

Experience from the world of therapy has raised awareness of the dangers of incompetent practitioners and, as a result, the national regulation of psychological therapies continues to be the subject of much discussion. Why would spiritual directors want to be less skilled, less informed, and less accountable than their secular colleagues? I do not hold the view that to be "professional" in any way negates the possibility of acknowledging the charismatic quality of spiritual direction and in no way do I see them as mutually exclusive. Embracing a charism goes hand in hand with a commitment to exercise it responsibly and intelligently in response to the outpouring of God's generosity.

Christian teaching would seem to support the view that any work, whether teaching, psychotherapy, or spiritual direction, can be a calling from God, a vocation. I do not, therefore, consider that when I am working as a therapist or teacher, God is any less present than when I am working as a spiritual director. It therefore follows that I yearn to be the best teacher, therapist, or director that I can be and that I draw on my faith and my relationship with God in all areas of my work. I also have cause to reflect on the parable of the talents and the fact that I am accountable for how I use my gifts (Matthew 25:14–30; Luke 19:12–28), although I am only too aware that I often fall short of the ideal.

Because of this sense of vocation, it is impossible for me to separate one calling from another. I hold myself accountable to my aspiration to use the gifts God has given me in His service. I do not believe that He privileges the gifts that I use when I am with a spiritual directee over and above those that I use when I am in other contexts. And it is my belief that the more I immerse myself in this vocation to which I feel called—through experience, reflection, training, and study— the more I grow and develop and the more I become the person God made me to be. Whenever I hear a spiritual director talking negatively about the "over-professionalization" of spiritual direction and the dangers of losing the charism, I experience this hostility as demeaning and as a covert criticism of my role as a psychotherapist, teacher, or supervisor. When I am working with a client who, despite an experience of acute depression, is becoming increasingly able to function in the world and who is beginning to feel restored to life, then I am reminded of St Irenaeus' assertion that "The glory of God is a person fully alive". I believe that the qualities I need for my work in these roles are every bit as much a charism as those I need to do my work in the role of spiritual director. The Bible may specifically mention healing, preaching, and teaching as gifts from God but it is my belief that these may all be observed in the practice of spiritual direction.

It is often in the area of ethics and boundaries that the fear of "professionalization" is expressed, which makes me wonder what the fear might *really* be about. In considering this question, it may be helpful to identify differences in current practice between the two disciplines and to explore the question of whether these differences should be maintained.

Initial covenant/contract

The initial contract, or covenant, is an important starting point. While therapists pay a great deal of attention to what information must be given to clients at the outset, in spiritual direction there often seems to be less clarity and consensus, and the content and structure of the initial meeting may be much more fluid than would generally be the case in therapy. However, it seems essential that basic boundary issues are addressed at this point in the relationship.

The initial contract between therapist and client will establish regular, and relatively frequent, days and times to meet, and the limits of confidentiality will be explained; both directees and psychotherapy clients can expect the length and frequency of sessions to be discussed and established and, if relevant, how much they will cost. Both will also expect to be informed about the consequences, if any, of missed appointments and the whole issue of confidentiality will be addressed. Both directors and therapists will clarify how available they may (or may not) be between sessions, either by telephone, email, or letter.

Many spiritual directors would see some or most of the above as unnecessary and irrelevant and might even be hostile to the use of the word "contract" to describe this initial working agreement. In my therapy work I am very conscious that the formation of an early therapeutic alliance, and therefore a positive outcome to the therapy, is often dependent on just such an initial contract, in which clear and mutual expectations can be established. I therefore do not see why this should be different in the case of the relationship between director and directee. We are talking about process as well as content here, and clarity is essential for both parties to be able to make an informed choice about whether they work together or not.

Confidentiality

In the case of therapy, information regarding confidentiality will depend on the setting in which it takes place, for example, whether in private practice, in the public sector, such as schools or GPs' surgeries, or in a charitable agency. Therapists are expected to know both the legal position regarding the mandatory breaking of confidentiality in accordance with the Prevention of Terrorism Act (2000) and the Proceeds of Crime Act (2002), and also the policy relating to procedures for safeguarding children and vulnerable adults, and working with clients who are at risk of suicide. They would also be expected to be informed about the possible charge that evidence might be contaminated in the event of a court case and be able to deal with this appropriately. The situation regarding supervision and the keeping of notes and records would also be addressed.

Many spiritual directors would be uncomfortable addressing all the above topics, feeling that to do so would lead to an over-legalistic atmosphere. But avoiding these issues may result in extreme complications should the subjects arise at some point in the future. While a director working privately may not be legally obligated to break confidentiality, ethical considerations must be taken into account, and the rules for those working under the authority of the church are quite clear. For example, if a directee mentions the fact that she was sexually abused as a child by a relative who still has access to children, or that she is seriously considering suicide, then the director cannot ignore this information and must make choices and decisions about what action, if any, to take. Ethical practice indicates that it is beneficial to address the boundaries and limitations of confidentiality at the outset of the relationship. Once the proverbial cat is out of the bag, it cannot be returned—we cannot *not* know what we have been told just because we don't know what to do about it. When a spiritual director is a priest, then there is the added complication that formal confession and absolution may be part of the session, in which case confidentiality to the directee is assured under Proviso to Canon 113 of the Code of 1603, part of the Canon Law of the Church of England, which remains in force despite various modern revisions. While there are, doubtless, many spiritual directors who are every bit as well informed as therapists on the above issues, there are many for whom it would all come as unwelcome and surprising news.

It therefore seems clear that there are differences in understanding about the nature of confidentiality between therapy and spiritual direction. I suspect that this has grown out of the particular culture of faith communities, where those in positions of leadership may in the past have expected to be kept more fully informed of what is happening in the lives of members of their congregations than would be the case elsewhere. Of course this raises the whole question of whether directors should be seeing directees from within their own congregations at all. In my view, it is definitely undesirable, but I am aware that many people still consider it to be acceptable practice. Changes in culture take time, but while this practice continues, the related issue of dual relationships becomes particularly pressing and relevant.

Dual relationships

Such relationships may occur when director and directee find that their paths cross in contexts other than that of spiritual direction. Most obviously this arises when both are members of the same faith community, although even in this very specific example there may well be varying degrees of difficulty. In a very large congregation, of perhaps several hundred, or even thousand, members, two people may have little, if any, personal contact, whereas in a small community, the likelihood of overlap is high, and two people may even find themselves in the same house group, on the same committee, or involved in the same parish activities. However, when one of the parties has a formal and acknowledged leadership role in the community, it is hard to see how the director/directee relationship can be sustained without there being some effect on the dynamics between them. I would therefore see this situation as undesirable, unhealthy, and possibly even dangerous.

Of course it is also perfectly possible that two people living in the same geographical area—even if there is no contact within a faith setting—may come face-to-face with each other in some other context. For example, they may meet in the supermarket, or find themselves members of the same gardening club or regular users of the local swimming pool or gym. And this is also the case for therapists and their clients. In this we come back to the initial covenant or contract: good practice would suggest that the possibility of such a situation arising should at least be mentioned at the initial meeting and some agreement reached about the best way to deal with it.

Both spiritual directors and therapists face ethical problems when, in the course of their practice, they unwittingly realise that they know someone their client/directee is talking about. It is quite possible that this may arise in all sorts of circumstances, which may include overlap in their own personal life or may be through a more tenuous connection from information that has been brought by another client or directee. It can be difficult to know how best to respond ethically in this type of situation, and access to experienced and competent supervision is very important. However, in the case of spiritual direction, codes of practice are uncommon and supervision not mandatory.

Supervision

Expectations regarding supervision are very different between therapy and spiritual direction. While registered and accredited therapists are required to have adequate and appropriate supervision, spiritual directors are only advised to have some form of supervision in place, which may in practice mean being a member of a large group (eight to twelve participants) which meets only a few times a year. I am aware of spiritual directors who openly say that they don't need supervision because they talk things over with their spouse, thus showing not only a lack of understanding about the nature and importance of supervision, but also a total disregard for basic elements of confidentiality. However, the fact that supervision is seen as desirable at all is an encouraging step forward and the provision of supervision training courses is developing as awareness of the benefit for both directors and directees is being raised.

Self-disclosure

While a directee may reasonably assume that someone offering spiritual direction is a person of faith, this is not so in the case of psychotherapists and their clients. When prospective clients have any choice about who is to be their therapist, they may well ask about beliefs, values, and faith but, as is often the case in the health service and in many agencies, they will not always be given such a choice and may therefore be unsure about what response they may receive if they ask such a question.

Richards and Bergin suggest that therapists examine their attitudes towards the disclosure of their personal beliefs and values to their clients: "In attempting to help clients make healthy value choices, it may often be appropriate for therapists to openly but non-dogmatically share and discuss their own values" (1997, p. 135). This quotation relates to those therapists who have a particular faith, but I would also suggest that therapists who consider that any religious belief is evidence of pathology should be just as open with prospective clients, although I suspect that these practitioners would be unwilling to admit to holding such hostile views.

Notes and records

If notes and records are kept, then it is important that clients or directees are made aware that this is the case and how confidentiality is maintained. While there may in fact be considerable diversity in the methods that therapists adopt, there would seem to be a general expectation that in certain circumstances, for example, for legal reasons, therapists might well have to explain a complete absence of notes or records. When writing about the requirements of the British Psychological Society and the British Association for Counselling and Psychotherapy (BACP), Bond & Mitchels comment: "Not to keep records would require justification" (2008, p. 57). Common practice would suggest that many therapists keep anonymous notes that state, quite factually, the main issues that have been explored in each session. They may also maintain a cross-referencing system, which would include contact details, number of sessions attended and payments made, and which would be kept separately. Currently there is no evidence to suggest that the same applies to spiritual directors, but equally there is no evidence to suggest that the same does not apply, so it would seem helpful for directors to reflect on the possible situations that could arise and to make a conscious decision about what explanation they would give if they were challenged to explain the lack of any notes or records. If it is considered good practice for therapists to be accountable in this way, then it would seem reasonable, whether or not there is a legal requirement to do so, for spiritual directors to adopt the same standards. It is, obviously, also essential to keep accurate records of payments made for income tax purposes.

Limits of competence and issues of referral

In the interests of ethical practice and client safety, it is vital that therapists and spiritual directors are able to recognise the limits of their own competence and are willing to engage with those with whom they work to access appropriate levels of help when necessary. This is usually relatively easy for therapists who are members of a professional body and who will have their own network of colleagues and fellow-professionals they can turn to for advice. There is also a wide body of written material which can support therapists in exploring particular topics. Spiritual directors may not have such resources easily available, and may not find themselves in an environment with a culture which encourages such networking.

An important aspect of being able to recognise the limits of our own competence arises when we become aware that we are not in a good enough state physically, psychologically, emotionally, or spiritually to continue working, at least for the time being, either as therapists or directors. Adequate self-care is required of therapists, who are expected to pay attention to all aspects of their own well-being so that they can spot vulnerabilities and danger signs before the possibility that these become detrimental to the interests of their clients. In contrast to this attitude, the history and culture of spiritual direction may exacerbate a tendency to "keep going" and to pay little attention to personal needs, which may even be seen as self-indulgence. It can be out of this misunderstood sense of duty to their directees, to the church, and even to God, that burnout develops. Without sufficient self-resourcing, directors become at best stale, and at worst dangerous. When we lose touch with the very real evidence of what is happening to us through our body's response to circumstances, how can we stay in touch with God's will for us, with the Holy Spirit's mysterious presence, and with

Jesus' saving grace? Our duty to our God, to our directees—and to ourselves—is to monitor our well-being, not as self-indulgence, but to sustain us as safe and ethical practitioners.

In this connection, Ruffing draws our attention to the value of supervision: "Because of the nature of spiritual direction, supervision is not merely a psychological process, but a spiritual one as well. Directors are profoundly affected by directees" (2000, p. 169). In addition to regular supervision, perhaps one of the best ways to support ourselves is through our own spiritual direction or therapy. To present ourselves to another on a regular basis, openly and authentically, to be willing to examine our own emotional experience and to explore the effect we have on others, will help us to work through our own vulnerabilities and thus be more available to those whom we seek to serve.

Prayer

Expectations around prayer will usually form part of the initial discussion in spiritual direction—perhaps the session will start with silence and end with extempore or formal prayer depending on the directee's personal preference—and directors may also explain how they see their own commitment to praying for directees between sessions. In most circumstances this would not be the case in therapy. For many therapists, praying either with or for a client would never be part of the counselling process and this whole question is explored further in Chapter Eight.

Continuing professional development

On-going training and professional development is perhaps one of the areas of greatest difference between psychotherapy and spiritual direction. As in many professions, the requirement for formalised continuing professional development is now well-established in the therapy world and is beginning to gain ground in the spiritual direction context, although, as was once the case in therapy, there are many directors who have no formal training and who do not engage in any regular and specific process of improving and developing their knowledge and skills.

Resistance to professional development may arise out of a sense of insecurity and may be another example of reluctance to move towards what has already been described as "over-professionalization". But, as our awareness of the psychological complexity of human nature grows, together with the development of our understanding of neuroscience, and as interest in spiritual direction also grows, any reluctance to being well informed and well equipped to address complex issues must be considered irresponsible and unethical.

Money matters

One of the main differences in practice for therapists and spiritual directors has, at least in the past, been the issue of charging and payment. In the main, therapists in independent practice charge, although many have a sliding scale and some may offer *pro bono* sessions for clients with genuine financial difficulties. In the case of agencies, the policy varies, often depending on their charitable status and, again, there may be a sliding scale. While the decision about whether and how much to charge is often based on pragmatic considerations about the actual cost of providing therapy, there is also the justification that clients need to have investment in their own development and that they won't value what they don't pay for.

This has not been the case with spiritual directors who, traditionally, have not charged for their services and in many cases still do not do so, largely because in the past directors were clergy who were already receiving a stipend and therefore indirect, if not direct, payment. As the number of lay people acting as directors increases, the practice of charging is becoming more common. However, there are those who consider that they have "freely received" and should therefore "give freely" of their time and talents and see this as a Biblical injunction (Matthew 10:8). While this stance obviously has great integrity, it could be seen as discriminatory, with the result that, ultimately, only those with sufficient financial means can offer spiritual direction, particularly when the cost of supervision, travel, and on-going training are taken into account.

The whole question of charging is, for many people, a contentious one and I suspect that some of the reluctance to charge for spiritual direction arises from the director's personal discomfort at raising and addressing the issue of money with directees. I would therefore suggest that directors might reflect on the underlying philosophy and theology of their decisions around this point and explore and examine their own sense of self-worth in order to become clearer about the origins of their reluctance. They may discuss the whole subject in their own spiritual direction or in supervision and may still come to the conclusion that they do not wish to charge, but then their decision would be based on increased self-awareness rather than on a fear of addressing the tricky issue of money.

It would seem both helpful and ethical to raise the subject of payment at the initial contact stage with a prospective directee. Perhaps the most important factor when considering payment is that all parties need to be honest with themselves and with each other about what has integrity for them and what they are willing and able wholeheartedly to commit to. This seems to me to be satisfactory at all levels, and also practical and sustainable for both participants. It also seems unlikely that avoiding the issue will bode well for open and honest dialogue about other subjects that may arise in the course of the spiritual direction relationship.

For further considerations about the pros and cons of receiving fees or charges for spiritual direction, see Silver (2003, pp. 23–35).

Insurance

It is not uncommon for spiritual directors to consider that professional indemnity insurance for their work is completely unnecessary—a reflection of their reluctance to become professionally accountable to their directees and to the wider community. Clergy, and some laity authorised by their own faith communities, may be covered by overarching policies, but this isn't necessarily the case, and practitioners would be unwise to make any assumptions without checking their personal position. They can then make their own arrangements for insurance if necessary.

Professional indemnity insurance is now available for spiritual direction and for spiritual coaching with major insurance providers.

Legal issues

I have often heard spiritual directors claim that legal considerations that apply to therapists do not apply to them. The refrain "But I'm not a therapist" is a common one which I'm afraid always rings warning bells for me. While the ethical imperative of maintaining good practice is obvious, there may be legal implications as well. I do not understand how, if something is considered unethical practice in one context, it can be considered as anything different in another. Gubi quotes one of his interviewees as follows: "if we believe, as I do, that in the relationship between counsellor and client the unconscious process will make a difference and therefore the counsellor can do damage to the client, why would that be any different with a spiritual director? … the process is the same" (2010, p. 45).

One of the areas which I consider may fall into the category of legal issues, is that of the possibility of contaminating evidence in cases of sexual and other abuse that are subsequently brought to court; another is the question of what aspects of adoption may safely be explored with a professional who is not registered with the appropriate statutory body. I have on several occasions asked supervisees about what action they would take if the issue of childhood sexual abuse were to arise in spiritual direction: the answer has been that they would seek the help of those, appointed by their church, involved in safeguarding children and vulnerable adults, with the implication being that this would then be the end of the matter from their point of view. While this may be the correct initial action to take, directees may still need the support of their director, and the whole question of the dangers of contamination of evidence may then be relevant.

Spiritual directors need to be mindful of the dangers of discussing details of abuse in the process of direction if there is any possibility that a court case may at some time in the future ensue. Bond & Sandhu remind us that "avoiding the contamination of witness evidence is a high priority in the delivery of fair trials. Contamination can lead to false convictions as well as false acquittals. Discussion with witnesses prior to trials have led to both these outcomes" (2005, p. 91), and they go on to state:

> Therapy is viewed by courts *as only one of many forms* of pre-trial discussion that can adversely affect a fair trial. The main concern with regard to pre-trial discussions of any kind is the potential impact on the reliability of the evidence of the witnesses and the difficulty it creates in court in being able to determine the weight to be given to that evidence. (ibid., p. 92, italics mine)

In the case of adult directees, the director needs to inform them that, in the event of legal proceedings, the prosecution could claim that the evidence has been contaminated, and then it is for the directee to decide whether they wish to continue to explore this material. In the case of children who cannot make this decision for themselves, the material should not be addressed (although it is worth making the point that not many children are engaged in spiritual direction so in reality it is unlikely that such a situation would often arise).

While therapy trainings will address such legal considerations and the procedures that may arise in court, this does not seem to be so in spiritual direction trainings. If it emerges that a witness in a trial has been receiving spiritual direction, it seems to me that there would be no reason why this situation might not similarly be used in an attempt to discredit the alleged victim's evidence. As Bond & Sandhu write:

> It is always in the defence's interest within an adversarial criminal trial to seek to discredit any evidence against a defendant and any ill-focused or poorly disciplined pre-trial therapy sessions are easy targets for allegations of "coaching" with the effect of partially or wholly undermining the evidence. (2005, p. 92)

There seems to be little awareness in the spiritual direction community of potential difficulties around working with issues of adoption and associated legal requirements. Whether or not the activity of spiritual direction would legally be considered in the same light as psychotherapy in relation to working with adoption, it would seem wise for directors to be sufficiently well informed of the potential psychological pitfalls of addressing such issues in depth with their directees in order that they can assess their own competence to practise in this area. And, whatever the legal position, if something is seen as potentially damaging for therapy clients, then why would the same not be true for spiritual directees?

I have come across an example of a relatively experienced spiritual director addressing issues relating directly to the question of adoption in some detail with an adopting parent with absolutely no awareness either of the complexity of the subject or of the potential legal minefield that she was entering. Gordon puts the case clearly when she states: "Since the passing, in December 2005, of amendments to the 2002 Children Act, it has been illegal, without government registration as an adoption support agency (ASA), to counsel anyone for whom any aspect of adoption is a main focus" (2010, p. 4). While spiritual directors could insist that they are not offering therapy, and that therefore this law doesn't apply to them, it may be considered that, if exploration of this material is likely to be detrimental to a psychotherapy client, then it is equally likely to be detrimental to a spiritual directee. In my experience, many spiritual directors are totally unaware of any possible psychological, ethical, or legal difficulties in this area.

Codes of ethical practice

While Spiritual Directors International have established their own Code of Ethics (www.sdiworld.org), and some Anglican diocese in the UK have a code of practice for spiritual directors, as yet there are no generally accepted guidelines of good practice, nor, it seems to me, are there likely to be unless and until some form of national association is formed. However, while an accepted code of practice is obviously desirable, unless this is coupled with procedures for sanctions in the event of a breach, then the effectiveness of such a code will obviously be limited. To establish, manage, and monitor a formal complaints procedure is a considerable task in terms of time, energy, expertise, and money.

However, the United Kingdom Council for Psychotherapy (UKCP) provides a statement of Ethical Principles and Code of Professional Conduct for registered psychotherapists, together with a number of documents and factsheets setting out policies and standards of practice in specific areas and these could also seem to be helpful in considering ethical issues in the practice of spiritual direction. The British Association for Counselling and Psychotherapy (BACP) has moved from the perhaps more legalistic and rigid set of rules suggested by a Code of Practice to the more flexible approach of the Ethical Framework for Good Practice in Counselling and Psychotherapy (2010), which would also be helpful when considering ethical issues in spiritual direction.

Summary

While there are many similarities in terms of the process of therapy and of spiritual direction, there are, nonetheless, many differences in current practice. Some of these differences emerge from their historical context, for example, attitudes towards payment and prayer. However, the reluctance of some spiritual directors to become "professional" may be as a result of a fear that their practice may be shown in an unfavourable light because of lack of knowledge and training: I would encourage such reluctant directors to be willing to explore and examine their own practice and to learn from the best of the conventions that are accepted by therapists.

When all is said and done, client/directee safety is the most important consideration, no matter what the setting or the intention behind the action or events. It is simply not satisfactory to project the responsibility for the outcome on to the Holy Spirit, denying our own part and failing to take responsibility for our own contribution. If the interests of the client are paramount, then spiritual directors have a positive duty to learn about what constitutes good practice in other, allied, disciplines. We cannot claim that the Holy Spirit will guide and protect us if we are not willing to make any attempt to ensure that we are practising safely and ethically. In fact I would suggest that, as professing Christians, there is an even greater responsibility to adopt the highest possible standards and continually to subject our practice to the most rigorous scrutiny. With this as the basis for all that we do, it is incumbent upon us to act only in a way that is consistent with what is currently known of modern psychology and with recent developments in neuroscience.

I would maintain that, in becoming more professional in terms of training, supervision, and accountability, in attempting to introduce national standards of competence, and in encouraging debate and discussion about what constitutes good practice, we are moving closer to what I would understand to be God's will for us and for our directees.

CHAPTER SEVEN

Power in the encounter

"The so-called psychiatric 'disorders' are nothing to do with faulty biology …
They are the creation of the social world in which we live, and that world is structured by power"

—David Smail

Introduction

I believe that relationship is at the heart of the practice of both psychotherapy and spiritual direction. In therapy, the central relationship is between client and therapist, and, while in spiritual direction it is between God and directee, the significance of the relationship between director and directee should not be underestimated. The recognition of the primacy of the relationship raises vital questions around issues of power within these relationships; as Mcleod points out: "Dilemmas and issues around the nature of power and control are intrinsic to counselling, for both counsellor and client" (1998, p. 378). In the case of spiritual direction—with its more authoritarian origins—it seems that this gets little attention. This chapter will examine issues of power that may arise, how they may play out in various types of therapy as well as in spiritual direction, and what questions therapists and directors might ask themselves about their own practice.

Power in the United Kingdom

An imbalance of power in any relationship is a reflection of the culture and ethos of the community in which it exists, and issues of power and oppression are specific to, and affected by, the society where they are to be found. History and social constructs determine where, and with whom, power and authority lie, and individuals may feel impotent in effecting significant change to the prevailing culture. When all the power seems to be vested in external systems, it is hard for individuals to develop a sense of self-agency or to have confidence in their ability to make a difference.

In contrast, at a human, personal, and individual level, psychotherapy seems to be offering empowerment, although, as we shall see, the truth of such a claim is worth considering when the balance of power between therapist and client (and also between director and directee) is more closely examined. It is therefore important to reflect on the context of the United Kingdom in the early years of the twenty-first century when thinking about these matters and to consider to what extent power is embedded in the fabric of society.

Despite some change in the system of inherited seats in the House of Lords, the government of the UK still does not have an elected second chamber and it is worth noting that certain Church of England bishops—necessarily male—hold seats by right of their position. Privilege continues and inherited power is still in evidence in the hands of a small and unelected section of the population. Institutions, including the state and the church, hold external power against which the individual is pretty well power*less*.

In the second half of the twentieth century legislation was introduced to ensure equality under the law in terms of race, sexual orientation, gender, and age. However, while the law may regulate against such overt discrimination, there remains much covert and, in some cases, institutionalised discrimination, not least within religious communities, where a hierarchical gulf between ordained and lay members can be seen, together with notable discrimination between the well-educated and the not-so-well-educated—not to mention the sexual inequality and homophobia that is still enshrined in many churches.

An increase in external power is also evident in recent developments in the world of therapy. In a climate where outcome measurement, empirical evidence, and "scientific" results are privileged—and funding is often dependent upon them—it is hard to claim that the increase in clients' self-agency can be identified as the primary goal. For example, government funding is given to drug and alcohol agencies on the basis of their positive outcome statistics, and attendance at therapy may be a condition of a court order in order to avoid a custodial sentence. It does not seem unreasonable to assume that such clients will see the agencies as part of the external authority "system" rather than as agents of personal empowerment.

Power in psychotherapy

The same power dynamics may well be found in the provision of therapy under the Increasing Access to Psychological Therapies (IAPT) programme, where funding will be conditional upon meeting targets: it will also be present in Employee Assistance Programmes (EAPs), where the goal is to ensure the employee's ability to be fully functioning in the work place. Equally, this emphasis on desired outcomes can be seen in therapeutic services in further and higher education, where student retention and achievement statistics are part of the performance criteria under scrutiny when funding is being allocated. Whenever and wherever clients are not paying for their own therapy, a question of power and an imperative for "good" outcomes will be in the frame, either consciously or unconsciously. As McCleod states: "In reality, questions of power and powerlessness are always present in counselling: in the stories told by the client, in the counsellor-client relationship and in the relationship between both counsellor and client and the counselling organisation" (1998, p. 379).

Masson, well-known for his suspicions and criticisms of therapy, comments that Freud believed that analysis was "a situation where there is a superior and a subordinate" (1997, p. 41) and later states his unequivocable view that "The therapeutic relationship *always* involves an imbalance of power" (ibid., p. 290, original italics). Masson would go so far as to claim that the therapeutic relationship is *of itself* abusive and asserts that "It is the world of therapy, it is *therapy* itself that is at the core of the corruption I have described" (ibid., p. 296).

Hawkins and Shohet (2006, p. 112), when writing about the supervisory relationship, identify three specific types of power which can, I think, just as well relate to the client/therapist or to the director/directee relationship:

Role power, which derives from the power inherent in the role in its organisational context. As already mentioned, in many church communities power is vested in those who are ordained by what is seen to be the ontological difference, that is, a difference in the very nature of being, between clergy and laity.

Cultural power, which derives from the dominant social and ethnic group, for example, white, male, heterosexual, able-bodied, educated, ordained.

Personal power, which derives from the particular power of the individual, both in terms of their level of expertise and the impact of their personality, evident, for example, in all charismatic leaders.

McLeod (1998, p. 240) describes Rogers (1978, p. 14) as regarding personal power as the reverse of authority power, developing from within rather than from external factors.

Each of the above types of power can, of course, be in evidence independently, but the cumulative effect of the power dynamic will obviously be even greater if there is a combination of more than one of these types of power present in a relationship. For example, the power present between therapist and client when the director is male, charismatic, white, heterosexual, able-bodied, and educated may be overpowering in a relationship with, say, a black, female, gay, disabled client with little education. If the power imbalance is extreme in these particular circumstances, how much more would it be in the case of a spiritual direction relationship if the director is also ordained, with all the authority and power inherent in the role of priest, and the directee is a member of the laity?

In exploring the balance of power in the relationships between client and therapist, director and directee, it is worth considering Buber's ideas about the nature of the encounter between two people and how such relationships may be experienced by both parties.

Buber's construct of the "I-Thou" experience suggests an encounter with the other as being of a significantly deep nature, embodying mutuality and equality, which can be sustained even in the absence of the other. The very word "Thou" implies the existence of the "I" as speaker—there can be no *thou* unless there is also *I*. Buber says, "The *Thou* meets me through grace—it is not found by seeking. ... But I step into direct relation with it" (1958, p. 11). Much has been written about I-Thou moments in the literature of therapy, but there seem to be nuances of meaning in the term and not much attention is paid to Buber's assertion that it is not found by seeking but through grace, (that is, through a mysterious supranatural experience that offers healing and growth). Conversely, the expectation and acceptance that grace is implicit in the spiritual direction process would be assumed by both directors and directees, but there might not be any conscious recognition of this intersubjective moment of co-creation. As the French philosopher Levinas writes: "The I says 'you' to a You who, as an I, says 'You' to the I" (1998, p. 148) and he goes on to comment on Buber's writing: "It is in the extension of the I-Thou relationship and that of the social existence with man that, for Buber, the relation to God is produced" (ibid., p. 149). Perhaps the poetry of e e cummings expresses this particularly succinctly: "i am through you so i" (1991, p. 537).

Psychodynamic therapy

Historically, psychodynamic practitioners would have been seen in the role of the expert who, while maintaining an extremely boundaried position, would interpret what their clients (whom, significantly, they referred to as patients), brought to therapy and would then make a clinical diagnosis. Traditionally almost everything brought to therapy was considered in terms of transference and the decision about what was real, rather than transferential, lay with the therapist. However Maroda calls this "the impossible distinction" (2004, p. 97) and explores how thinking is changing in terms of how both patient and therapist understand the difference between the two, suggesting that the patient is better placed to decide what is real.

In Buber's terms, I would see this historical attitude as an "I-It" encounter, de-personalised, objectified, and disowned. The relationship between therapist and client was unequal, lacking any sense of mutuality, in which one person (the expert) offers their expertise and treatment to the (needy) other (the patient). Towards the end of the twentieth century, a change in position developed as a more relational way of working began to be privileged, in which equality and mutuality are seen as beneficial to the therapeutic outcome. For example, Balint's view was that:

> The more the analyst's technique and behaviour are suggestive of omniscience and omnipotence, the greater is the danger of a malignant form of regression. On the other hand, the more the analyst can reduce the inequality between the patient and himself, and the more unobtrusive and ordinary he can remain in his patient's eyes, the better are the chances of a benign form of regression. (1968, p. 173)

Maroda notes "the value of establishing a mutual, reciprocal, and non-authoritarian relationship between therapist and patient to facilitate an optimal treatment outcome" (2004, p. 6). However, it is still worth asking whether mutual necessarily means equal in these circumstances.

It could be argued that Kohut, firmly grounded in the psychoanalytic tradition and one-time president of the prestigious American Pyschoanalytic Association, has had the greatest influence in providing a bridge between psychodynamic and humanistic practice at the beginning of the twentieth century and that of the twenty-first century. Kohut (1971), with Gill, raised the whole question of the centrality of the relationship between client and therapist. He noted that the techniques that hitherto he believed had supported his practice were not always adequate and he developed the notion that the infant needs to experience mirroring (parental acceptance, love, and approval), idealisation (someone to look up to, to have confidence in), and twinship (someone as a role model). He called this theory of developmental relating "Self-psychology", which enabled many psychodynamic practitioners to have more in common with the beliefs of the humanistic practitioners who were gaining ascendancy in the United States in the aftermath of the second world war. As Kahn says:

> Traditionally this stance has been seen as the direct opposite of the psychoanalytic position, with its notions of the unconscious, resistance and defence, all of which imply that clients know little about themselves. And now here is a psychoanalyst teaching that clients know what they need a good deal better than their therapist, and that the therapist would do well to listen carefully and attempt to grasp the client's experience empathically. (1997, p. 110)

Note the use of the word "client" rather than "patient" in this passage. There is recognition that the power is shifting, even for the psychoanalyst, and it is through working with the transference that the power can be dissolved and the client thus, ultimately, empowered.

The work of Daniel Stern, again coming from a psychodynamic background, explores infant development and observes the primacy of the relationship between mother and child, which he describes in considerable detail, that lays the foundation for all other relationships. Infant observation studies show just how much babies contribute to the wordless dialogue that constitutes communication between themselves and their caregivers and Stern states that they "exert major control over the initiation, maintenance, termination and avoidance of social contact" (1985, p. 21). This observation would suggest that infants are born with the capacity and desire for interrelatedness, are hardwired for relationship—they are not merely recipients in the communication between themselves and their caregivers but are active participants, and the relationship is truly dyadic.

When considering motivation for becoming a therapist, Maroda (2004), drawing on the writings of Bollas (1987), examines the desire in therapists not only to enable the patient to be transformed but to be transformed themselves through the therapeutic encounter. She writes that Bollas speaks of "every person's desire to be transformed and the regularity with which this is expressed in the pursuit of religion, transcendent aesthetic experiences and, of course, relationships" (1987, p. 38), suggesting a strong sense of mutuality and potential for co-created transformation in the therapeutic relationship. Maroda goes so far as to suggest that, for therapy to be truly effective, therapist and patient need to share madness, pain, and vulnerability (2004, p. 55).

Cognitive behavioural therapy (CBT)

The very use of the word "patient" rather than "client" gives a clear message that denies any sense of mutuality and equality of relationship and it is interesting that in the 2007 government initiative Increasing Access to Psychological Therapies (IAPT), with its emphasis on Cognitive Behavioural Therapy, the word "patient" is the label of choice, reflecting the medical roots of this particular approach of therapy.

CBT practitioners work on the basis that patients' thinking is distorted and that, if this distortion can be corrected, a beneficial outcome in terms of mood and behaviour can be achieved. The emphasis is very much on reality checking and finding the rational view or explanation which may not always take into account relative attitudes to events. This suggests that, in many circumstances, there is a "right" or a "wrong" answer and this model of therapy claims to have scientific validity because the results are measured using "objective" outcome instruments.

Proctor (2002) explores the question of power within a CBT relationship in which the therapist is seen to hold a neutral position. The position of the participant/observer is examined and Proctor demonstrates the power implicit in the role of the practitioner who "knows" what the desired outcome within the CBT framework should be. She goes on to say: "Given … that clients will seek therapy when in distress, their choices or resistance to the norms communicated by the therapist are likely to be very limited" and points out that, despite an avowal of the importance of collaboration between therapist and client,

> it is clear that the "collaborative" relationship emphasises the therapist's expectations of the client, that the client will contribute to the therapist's ideas and plans for treatment (within the CBT model). While some things are perhaps negotiable, there are clearly some aspects of CBT that the patient must agree to for the therapy to go ahead. (2002, p. 71)

Thus, while the notion of "collaboration" is introduced, the power remains very much with the therapist.

Humanistic and integrative therapy

In humanistic therapy, the role of the therapist is to enter into the world of the client (not patient), to be attuned to the client's experience, and, together, to co-create meaning in an intersubjective framework. However, this does not eliminate any possibility of a power imbalance and West observes that "person-centred counsellors and psychotherapists (and humanistic therapists in general) often seem to underestimate the power relationship between client and therapist" (2000, p. 70), and Mearns & Cooper point out that "there is a very narrow boundary between encountering and invading" (2005, p. 103).

Carl Rogers, the founder of person-centred counselling (PCC), saw therapy as a method of working with people where the client retains personal power and responsibility. This belief would seem to encapsulate both the purpose and the process of therapy. Rogers stated that "the politics of the client-centred approach is a conscious renunciation or avoidance by the therapist of all control over, or decision-making for, the client. It is the facilitation of self-ownership by the client" (1978, p. 14 in Mcleod, 1998, p. 248). As McCleod comments: "Ultimately this is a form of power based in love rather than in fear" (1998, p. 240).

Rogers' underlying philosophy was one in which the aim was equality between therapist and client. In seeking to make the process of therapy much more accountable and transparent, Rogers was aware that his approach was radically different from that of traditional therapy and said that criticism of person-centred counselling arose "primarily because it struck such an outrageous blow to the therapist's power" (Proctor, 2002, p. 90). However, the emphasis was on the role of the therapist in the therapeutic relationship, rather than on the examination of the contributions of both therapist and client in the co-creation of the intersubjective dialogue. Mearns and Cooper make the distinction between a uni-directional model of relatedness from therapist to client and a bi-directional model of mutual relatedness between therapist and client as follows: "We can distinguish between 'presence' as a coming together of congruence, empathy and acceptance at high levels in the therapist; and 'relational depth', which requires both the presence of the therapist, and *some form of presence or responsiveness from the client*" (2005, pp. 43–44, original italics). They also make the point that relational depth exists outside times of proximity (ibid., p. *xii*), an important fact for both therapists and directors to remember.

In order to be able to say that the relationship is truly mutual, we need to examine the role of the client in the co-creation of that relationship. A great deal has been written on the subject of how the therapist expresses what Rogers' identified as the core conditions of empathy, unconditional positive regard, and congruence, and how the client experiences them, but I am also interested in the client's contribution of these conditions in the intersubjective relationship with the therapist. So, while Rogers' person-centred model of working with clients certainly demonstrates a major shift away from the traditional view of "therapist as expert", it can still be argued that, at least implicitly, power lies with the therapist. Certainly Buber, in conversation with Rogers, maintained that, in the therapeutic relationship, the therapist always maintains the power:

> Buber: A man coming to you for help. The essential differences between your role in this situation and his is obvious. He comes for help to you. You don't come for help to him. And not only this, but you are able, more or less, to help him. He can do different things to you but not help you … he is foundering around, he comes to you …. You are not equals and cannot be. (Kirschenbaum & Henderson in West 2000, p. 30)

Bozarth, writing on the same dialogue, quotes Rogers on the subject of the therapeutic relationship as follows: "This is something immediate, equal, a meeting of two persons on an equal basis, even though, in the world of I-It, it could be seen as a very unequal relationship" (Bozarth in Proctor 2002, p. 93). As Mearns & Cooper, seeking to explore the differentiation between the uni-directional and bi-directional models of therapy mentioned above, state: "Within the person-centred field, there is also a tendency to focus on the therapist's experiences and communications *towards* the client … rather than the bi-directional, mutual encounter *between* therapist and client" (2005, p. 14, original italics). However, the development of more relational models of therapy recognises that empathic attunement is a two-way, rather than a one-way, process, and that the therapist too is changed by the encounter. In accepting that the therapeutic process is bi-directional, therapist power is reduced and a more mutual environment can be co-created.

Power in spiritual direction

Traditionally (with the notable exception of The Society of Friends) Christian church institutions have been hierarchical and authoritarian. Even in the twentieth century, when learning theory acknowledged the benefits of more collaborative teaching styles, churches stayed with a didactic model of instruction and continue to offer sermons and homilies, a model which encourages unquestioning acceptance of the received wisdom and discourages discussion and debate. In such circumstances, authority remains firmly with those specifically commissioned to hold power. It is perhaps not surprising therefore that, in a general climate of increasing individualism and faced with a church climate of authoritarianism, mainstream congregations have experienced a falling away of numbers. Unsurprisingly, therefore, it would seem that more individuals are seeking spiritual direction, which they experience as a safe space in which to explore their own journey of faith with someone who they hope will listen *to* them rather than preach *at* them.

However, the potential for power imbalance and lack of equality in the spiritual direction relationship is just as great as in the therapeutic relationship and many, if not all, of the issues already considered in this chapter may well be present. As already mentioned, the traditional areas of oppression—that is, of race, gender, sexual orientation, disability, and education—may in fact be even more relevant because they have still not been fully addressed in the life of Christian churches.

In the case of women, it is only in the last century that women have been accepted into the formalised leadership of many of the Christian denominations and this is still far from the case in the Roman Catholic church. It is perhaps worth noting that the Anglican church, which is the established church of the United Kingdom, only accepted women priests at the very end of the twentieth century and, nearly twenty years later, is still arguing about whether women can or may be ordained bishops. It is disappointing that certain sections of the Anglican church actually consider it necessary to identify themselves as "inclusive"—it is an indictment of any church that this is not the default position when it might properly be assumed that no church would want to be seen as "exclusive".

While some churches do fully accept gay Christians as members of their community, there are many that do not, and some that are actively hostile, stating that being gay is a sin in the eyes of God. Even those churches that claim to accept gays and lesbians are not quite so happy if they find that their clergy are gay and there are many examples of the "Don't ask, don't tell" policy—a collusive position which invites clergy to keep silent about their sexuality, effectively asking them to live a lie. In the Anglican church there is an expectation that gay clergy will remain celibate.

As well as the above areas of discrimination and oppression, there is also the historical class situation which is reflected in the verse of the well known hymn "All Things Bright and Beautiful"—"The rich man in his castle, the poor man at his gate/He made them high a lowly/He ordered their estate"—clearly stating that our position in society is divinely ordered and not to be challenged. While this verse is usually omitted these days, this is a relatively recent change and, in practice, few in church leadership will invite and encourage the more powerless members of the congregation to take an active role in their decision-making process.

In a climate where all the above is the daily experience, it is not hard to imagine that the unconscious messages that are still prevalent in the world of organised religion discourage a sense of equality and mutuality. The Christian church has been one of the most powerful institutions for two thousand years and throughout history people who have challenged and disagreed with it have found themselves persecuted, oppressed, isolated, or exiled—and at times tortured and executed. We may consider that we have moved on from the time of Galileo, the Inquisition, and the Reformation, yet subtle (and not so subtle) discrimination may still be found lurking under the surface.

Traditionally, although with a few notable exceptions such as Evelyn Underhill and Catherine Doherty, spiritual directors were priests (male) who already held positions of power and respect within their communities. The fact that, in faith communities with a strong tradition of spiritual direction, clergy still bear the title "Reverend" and are known as "Father" gives a powerful message about their status, particularly in churches that hold a theological view that ordination to the priesthood confers an ontological change, thus making a clear distinction between the very nature-of-being of clergy and that of laity. The whole question of whether absolution is offered by clerical spiritual directors raises questions of power that are only to be found in the spiritual direction context. The authority to forgive sins is, obviously, hugely powerful and sets up a unique dynamic between director/directee, and, personally, I cannot see how this can be dissolved in the spiritual direction relationship.

If spiritual directors have traditionally been priests, inherent in the relationship between them and their directees is a hierarchical distinction which must, by its nature, deny the possibility of mutuality and equality. If these beliefs are held by participants, then it is impossible for the power to be dissolved in the relationship. I would question whether, with these suppositions, either participant would even desire mutuality, preferring to see the director as wiser and more experienced in spiritual matters and consequently maintaining superior status.

In his book *Clericalism: The Death of Priesthood*, Wilson, a Jesuit priest, identifies unexamined attitudes and beliefs held by priests and by laity which help to maintain an imbalance of power that permeates the Roman Catholic church. For example:

Clergy: "Simply by our vocation as ordained ministers we are special-
          ists in the realm of the spiritual, and the laity aren't".
 Laity: "They're the pros in the things of God; we're just amateurs."
          (2008, p. 30).

Such unexamined attitudes give rise to deadly forms of clericalism, which Wilson explores in depth, highlighting the potentially disastrous results if this situation is allowed to continue unchallenged and unre-formed. He also examines the history of the sexual abuse tragedy in the Roman Catholic church, an example of the effects of unchecked power in an institution. His investigation is more philosophical and social than psychological and forensic, which seems to me to be a pity, uniquely placed as he is to have something useful to say in this area. However, he does point out that "With respect to the laity, the response ... focuses totally on measures for preventing future abuse ... it provides no deeper analysis of the cultural patterns that enabled the abuse in the first place" (ibid., p. 91). No doubt in the future, criminal psychologists will have much to say about the pathology of clergy perpetrators of sexual abuse.

Less extreme examples of misuse of power in spiritual direction can be seen when a director determines what constitutes a desirable out-come, for example, that a directee will return to or join a church com-munity or go on retreat or read a certain book. In such circumstances it is hard to see how a spirit of co-creation can exist to any significant degree.

In my practice as a supervisor of spiritual direction, I have certainly come across directors for whom this was clearly the case. One was a lay man called Vincent who was very involved in his local church and was seeing three directees, all of whom had been referred to him by his par-ish priest, at times when they were struggling with their faith in terms of organised religion. There were therefore already huge questions about hierarchy and power in the way in which this spiritual direction was entered into, by both director and directee. I became increasingly aware that Vincent felt he must encourage his directees to participate more fully in the local church, which he saw as "successful" spiritual direction. This left me in a quandary as I felt increasingly uneasy about being complicit in what I considered to be unethical practice. In the end Vincent's circumstances changed and I was relieved when he stopped seeing spiritual directees as he became more involved in other church activities.

Conclusion

Just as in the relationship between client and therapist, it is only when the power imbalance between spiritual director and directee is minimised and dissolved that a safe environment for significant growth can be co-created.

When approaching the question of power in spiritual direction and when reflecting on the inherent imbalance almost inevitable in church institutions, I have been struck by the fact that, *despite* this history of authoritarianism, in the main spiritual directees speak highly of their clergy spiritual directors, of what they offer, and of their personal relationship with them. With the potential for such a power imbalance as I have described above, it is perhaps both surprising and laudable that clergy are able to offer sensitive spiritual direction to laity at all. And yet, in my experience it is most certainly the case that they do. Taken at face value, this would seem to be an unlikely outcome, which leads me back to Buber's concept of the I-Thou encounter *which is graced by God*. I can, perhaps, hear some sceptical therapists rebutting such reports of positive experiences as emerging from a defended position in the directee and from unconscious desires to please, but I can only say that this is not at all my sense. What I hear is that something powerfully healing and life-giving happens in the encounter between director and directee, and, whether we conceptualise this as the work of the Holy Spirit or relate it to Buber's I-Thou concept, really doesn't matter. It is more important to be willing to keep an open mind, while at the same time rejoicing in the potential for growth and healing in the human spirit.

Many of the factors that promote imbalance of power in both therapy and spiritual direction arise out of lack of training and of knowledge and understanding of issues of difference, diversity, and oppression. Most therapy training programmes would pay attention to these subjects, even if this is not the case with spiritual direction courses.

There is also the danger that individual practitioners may address these questions at a theoretical and cognitive level but not fully internalise and integrate their meaning affectively and spiritually.

It is perhaps in supervision that many of the issues raised above can first be identified and addressed but, as already mentioned, while supervision is a requirement in the United Kingdom for all accredited therapists, this is not the case for spiritual directors, who may not even be receiving their own spiritual direction. However, as mentioned in Chapter Six, there is an increasing expectation for supervision and for personal direction, which can only have a beneficial effect on the quality of the provision of spiritual direction in the United Kingdom.

CHAPTER EIGHT

Spirituality in the therapy room—is it OK to pray?

"... prayer, by which term I understand no vain exercise of words, no mere repetition of certain sacred formulae, but the very movement itself of the soul, putting itself in a personal relation of contact with the mysterious power of which it feels the presence ..."

—William James (1985)

Introduction

One of the most contentious areas of discussion in the exploration of psychotherapy and spiritual direction is that of the practice of prayer. In this chapter I shall explore what the word "prayer" actually means, the historical view of its role, the evidence for its effectiveness, and the possible benefits and pitfalls of its incorporation into the practice of psychotherapy and spiritual direction. I shall also consider the spiritual practice and prayer life of psychotherapists and spiritual directors themselves.

What is prayer?

How do we define "prayer"? Is there a common understanding or definition? Once again we are faced with the difficulty of trying to describe with words something that is, in fact, indescribable and which reflects in some mysterious way the nature of our relationship, our encounter, with the Other, with God. As Richards and Bergin (1997, p. 202) point out, some form of prayer is advocated by most of the world faiths, although the form it takes may differ from one religion to another.

James (1985) alerts us to the idea that prayer is about relationship rather than activity, a theme that can be found in many definitions and descriptions and which, in my view, resonates with the emphasis that therapists place on the therapeutic relationship.

Green describes the essence of genuine prayer as "this desire to experience God, to get beyond merely knowing about him to truly loving him" (1979, p. 81), again addressing those aspects of prayer which lead us into the intimacy of true relationship.

Gubi defines prayer as "the word that describes that process of being in touch with a sense of transcendent inter- (or intra-) connectedness" (2008, p. 26). The idea of intra-connectedness links with the whole sense of God being found in all things, in all people, and perhaps it is in the process of getting in touch with this aspect of ourselves that our journey towards connection with the Other develops. Gubi summarises O'Donohue's description of prayer as follows: "Prayer is an ancient longing; it has a special light, hunger and energy ... it is an attempt to enter into harmony with the deeper rhythm of life ... Prayer issues from that threshold where soul and life interflow" (ibid., p. 27).

Benner writes about prayer as follows: "Attending to God's presence is prayer. Increasing one's attunement to the ever-present God is living a life of prayer. Worded prayers form part of such a life. But prayer is much more than worded prayers" (2002, p. 115). Benner also refers to the writings of Julian of Norwich as follows: "(She) describes the process of prayerful attentiveness to another as involving a continuous looking back and forth between God and the other person. Prayer attentiveness is prayer" (ibid., p. 169). This is a theme clearly demonstrated in the writings of the life of Br Lawrence, a seventeenth century French monk, of whom it is stated: "That with him the set times of prayer were not different from other times; that he retired to pray, according to the directions of his Superior, but that he did not want such retirement, nor ask for it, because his greatest business did not divert him from God" (2008, p. 11). (His "greatest business" included washing up in the monastery kitchens, which he admitted was an activity not altogether to his liking!)

If we therefore consider that prayer is any activity or process that develops and enriches our relationship with God, a relationship and a process rather than an act, then it can be argued that any spiritual practice can be considered as prayer.

Historical attitudes to prayer and therapy

Historically the world of therapy has, in the main, frowned on the use of prayer as an intervention or strategy, although some Christian and pastoral counsellors have always argued for its inclusion. This seems to have been a reflection of a wider disavowal of anything that might be considered "spiritual" being brought into the therapy room and, as has already been discussed in Chapter Three, there is evidence of a shift in perspective over the past decade or so.

Is prayer effective?

Swinton cites research that suggests that prayer can have an observable positive effect on those prayed for: "A number of randomized control trials have highlighted the possibility that intercessory prayer (i.e., prayer for others) can be beneficial for health in general and mental health in particular" (2001, p. 88). He goes on to describe two double-blind research projects (Byrd, 1988 and Harris et al., 1999), indicating a positive outcome for the patients who were prayed for, although he acknowledges that, because of the number of possible variables, more studies are needed to validate the results. However, if, as some evidence would seem to suggest, prayer has a positive effect on outcomes, then it could be argued that therapists have a duty to pray for their clients. Cook et al. (2009, p. 182) also refer to these two projects, but they go on to point out that Roberts et al. (2007) report that only three such trials are recorded on the Cochrane Committee database of all double-blind randomised controlled trials and that therefore no firm conclusion on the efficacy of prayer can be drawn.

There is also the question of the effect of praying on the therapist as well as on the client. Thorne states unequivocally:

> It is my contention—and experience—that the holding in mind of clients … on a regular basis can have a remarkable impact on the therapeutic relationship … This regular "holding" of clients—in many ways much akin to silent or intercessory prayer—because it

is part of a spiritual discipline is likely to have far-reaching effects in other areas of therapists' lives and to illumine all their relationships. (2002, p. 42)

Can I pray inside the therapy room? If not, why not?

If we take the above question literally, we are asking whether the therapist can pray before, during, or after therapy has taken place. I know many therapists who would consider the practice of prayer before a session, preferably in the therapy room, to be central to their way of working and who would always try to ground themselves in the presence of God before a session starts. I find that including this time of preparation in my working routine is always beneficial, both to me personally and, I believe, to the quality of the work that ensues.

The subject of praying during the psychotherapy session then arises but, before considering whether we talk with our clients about prayer, it might be helpful to consider how comfortable we are as human beings talking about prayer in any other context. Perhaps we may find it easier to talk about sex or other very personal issues than to talk about prayer and it seems to me that we need to be comfortable in reflecting on our own prayer life (or lack of it) and our willingness to engage in conversation about it before we can even consider addressing it with our clients. Is it something we would take to our personal therapy? If not, is that because of our own reluctance or because of that of our therapist? I would suggest that we need to take stock of our own experience and, as with any topic in therapy, to check how willing we are to address our own unprocessed issues before considering approaching those of our clients.

Praying with clients is certainly a controversial issue (Gubi, 2001, 2002, 2003, 2008; Koenig & Pritchett, 1998; Rose, 2002; Sperry, 2001; West, 2000; 2004), and even its advocates draw attention to the possible pitfalls and contraindications of adopting this type of intervention (Pargament, 2007; Richards & Bergin, 1997; Swinton, 2001).

Richards & Bergin express their reservations about therapists praying with clients, although they go on to say: "We are not saying that therapists should never pray with their clients during therapy sessions. Praying with clients may be more appropriate in some settings and with some types of clients than with others. For example, therapists who practice in religious settings ... may find that it is expected, comfortable and helpful to pray with clients" (2002, p. 204).

They also make a useful comparison between attitudes towards contemplation, meditation, and centring prayer, and therapeutic practices such as relaxation and mindfulness, whose roots may be in eastern religions but which are now considered to be mainstream in the therapy context in the United Kingdom. In doing so, they draw our attention to the need for knowledge and understanding of possible denominational differences in attitude to some of these practices and stress the importance of being willing to be led by the client: "therapists will need to rely heavily on their clients' input to help them select forms of contemplation, meditation and spiritual imagery with which clients feel comfortable" (ibid., p. 207).

However, Tan (in Moon & Benner) identifies possible pitfalls relating to the use of prayer in therapy as follows: "Misusing or abusing spiritual resources like prayer … thus avoiding dealing with painful issues in therapy" (2004, p. 191), and Gubi , in his research on therapists' attitudes towards prayer in therapy, notes that some respondents were against the use of prayer for a variety of reasons, including:

> Prayer can lead to collusion between counsellor and client, leaving remaining fundamental assumptions unexplored.
>
> Prayer can be an avoidance of having to do the "dirty" work (facing difficult personal issues).
>
> Prayer … can be defensive and dangerous because it can prevent counsellors from addressing interpersonal issues which they find difficult.
>
> Prayer can take responsibility away from "self". Some clients can take refuge in an external God who is always forgiving. This can distract the client from taking responsibility for themselves.
>
> Prayer can be a form of "delusional thinking" with incompetent practitioners. (2001, p. 58)

Conversely, however, if as therapists we deny our clients the opportunity for prayer when specifically requested, then are we doing our clients a disservice and are we possibly meeting our own needs and addressing our own agenda? Personally I am aware of several occasions when I have been quite clear with clients who have asked that our sessions start with prayer that this would not be possible and I feel I might now handle such a situation differently. Admittedly, I did explore with them what prayer meant for them before saying "no" but, in the end, the decision was mine and was, I am now sure, the result of a sense of prohibition that was present in all my trainings. With hindsight, I now consider that I was putting my own dogma and convictions before those of my client and that a more productive way forward would have been to invite further comment and reflection from the client in each case.

And what about praying covertly *for* clients in the therapy room as I did when working with Charles, who presented with issues centring on complex family relationships. He felt used, betrayed, and rejected. As the work progressed, Charles became more and more angry, demonstrating extreme rage, stating that he wanted revenge and even expressing a wish for the death of those who he felt had betrayed him. I did not find our sessions easy and I experienced his violent outbursts as highly disturbing. I found myself thinking about Charles a great deal between sessions, reflecting on anger management techniques and spending a lot of time on him in supervision. During and after one particularly explosive session, I prayed (covertly) for guidance on how to stay grounded and be fully present during the sessions in the face of this extreme and vengeful emotional violence. I was, frankly, almost unbelieving when he arrived at our next meeting saying that he now wanted contact with his family and that he was planning to communicate his desire for reconciliation with those from whom he had been estranged for several years. He now wanted to explore how to address this in therapy and the goal became to re-establish contact and develop the relationships that had been fractured for so long.

I could not account for this 180 degree turnaround and, while I am not necessarily suggesting that it was the direct result of prayer, I do ask myself what part the fact that I consciously held this distressed person in mind over a period of time may have played in the therapeutic process. Charles' change in attitude and affect has since been maintained and he is now able to attend and enjoy family gatherings and is developing new and genuine relationships with family members.

Does encouraging clients to pray turn therapy into something nearer to spiritual direction, as West (2000, p. 102) suggests? In therapy we so often explore what clients find helpful in order to harness these activities or processes in the interests of increased well-being. Why, then, might we not encourage prayer if it has been identified as a positive element in a client's life? In fact, I have done just that with several clients who have expressed quite clearly that prayer has been almost the only thing that seemed to have a positive effect on their depression. As a result,

I have encouraged them to pay more attention to it, just as I would with any other beneficial strategy, such as taking exercise, creative activities, or other forms of self-care.

The potential difficulties highlighted in the literature, and my own personal experience as both therapist and client, confirm my view that I should not raise the question of prayer with a client, nor do I inform them that I will pray for them between sessions. However, I have now moved to a position where, if a client raises the possibility of prayer, either in or out of the session, I will be more open-minded and pay more attention to what this truly means both for them and me.

Can I pray for clients outside the therapy room? If not, why not?

I have to admit to some ambivalence about the question of whether it is unethical to pray for a client outside the session without their knowledge or whether, as a therapist who considers herself to be a Christian, it is my duty to pray for all my clients. It is also important to consider how much the aim of covert prayer is in reality to support the therapist as well as an attempt to address the client's issues. Rose describes the experience that many therapists will recognise of feeling quite desperate about the work with a client and turning to God in our helplessness: "Praying can be a way of easing that tension and staying with the situation" (2002, p. 23).

Rose raises one of the questions in this dilemma as follows: "Even if the client is prayed for in private, there is a possibility that such prayer could be a form of unconscious influence on the other" (ibid., p. 11).

On the same subject, Dossey (1993, p. 74ff) proposes some very interesting ideas about the nature and efficacy of prayer as seen in the context of our understanding of quantum mechanics, although acknowledging the possible unconscious consequences of such prayer. He concludes that, overall, it is not unethical to pray for clients without their consent: "I would maintain that as long as our efforts are filled with compassion, caring and love, there is little reason to fear that our prayers for others without their consent are somehow unethical (ibid., p. 80). Magaletta & Brawer (1998) draw attention to the fact that some clients may not want their therapist to pray for them and discuss whether it is better always to gain client consent. Gubi's research, in which he explored the views of therapists on the subject of praying for their clients outside the therapy room, indicates that the majority of his sample felt there was nothing unethical as long as the intent was beneficent (2008, pp. 104–112).

Working with Carol was an example of this in my own practice. Carol came to me for an initial session, having made a serious suicide attempt resulting in several weeks in hospital as a psychiatric in-patient. When she was discharged, her psychiatrist expressed the opinion that she would benefit from psychotherapy and she came to me privately, stating quite clearly that she wasn't sure that she wanted to live. At the end of our initial session, she said she wasn't sure that she wanted to engage in therapy at all. However, a few days later she rang to say she would like another appointment and we agreed that initially the focus of therapy would be to explore strategies for self-support. After the next session, I was left with an overwhelming feeling of her vulnerability, a recognition that she might in fact kill herself, and a sense of hopelessness. Frankly, it was my opinion that she had been discharged prematurely and I expressed my concerns for her well-being in a letter to her psychiatrist.

This brief contact with Carol left me feeling sad and anxious and these feelings became the focus of my prayer in the following days. I was helped in this by my own spiritual director—also a therapist—and, through an unusually intense awareness of the life-giving energy of God's creation, I found that I was able to connect in a vibrant way with God's generosity, goodness, and grace which lifted the burdensome element of what I was experiencing and which in some mysterious way touched me at a particularly deep and significant level. I felt transformed. When I next met Carol a few days later, she too talked of being transformed and, while we were very much at the beginning of our work together, she was now expressing a desire and motivation to live, which meant that the work had the potential for a positive outcome. I was left with a sense of a miracle—the word used by both Carol herself and also by her psychiatrist when he next saw her.

Thorne writes of the longing for their clients' well-being that therapists may experience while maintaining a stance of neutrality about goals or outcomes: "... the therapist, while yearning for the client's good, imposes no direction upon the process and no pre-determined goals. This is a silent and passionate accompaniment without expectation but with absolute commitment to the client's evolution towards the fullness of being" (2002, p. 42).

While recognising all the possible pitfalls of praying either for, about, or with a client and being aware of the inherent dangers, I am drawn to the conclusion that the most significant factor in this question is that of the intention behind the prayer. If, after reflection and examination this can truly be said to be for the client's well-being, then it seems to be both a legitimate and ethical addition to the therapeutic process.

Prayer in spiritual direction

In spiritual direction prayer is often (but not always) routinely included in each session and for many directors and their directees it is central to the process of direction. Nevertheless, the principle of explicitly checking the directee's individual wishes would seem to be important so that no unfounded assumptions are made. Some directees want little or no explicit prayer, assuming the presence of the Holy Spirit in the session without the necessity for any overt expression. The lack of an agreed code of ethics for spiritual direction makes it difficult to identify what would be considered good practice and I fear that many directors make assumptions that are more a reflection of their own experience and preferences than of those of their directees.

While the primacy of the client's best interests is fundamental to therapeutic practice, it is not so clearly stated or understood in the practice of spiritual direction. If the directee wants to include prayer in the session, then it may be in a variety of formats, for example, keeping a period of silence at the beginning and/or end of the session; or the director and/or directee may pray aloud either with "formalised" prayer, for example, the Lord's Prayer or the Grace, or extempore prayer, possibly asking for a sense of God's presence and grace at the beginning or, towards the end, reflecting on what has been brought to the session.

While there may be an expectation that prayer is an implicit part of spiritual direction, some of the potential dangers of prayer in therapy already identified may be relevant here as well; for example, prayer may be used as a defence against examining difficult and painful issues either by the director or the directee, or there may be an unhelpful tendency to avoid accepting relevant and appropriate personal responsibility. The directee may use prayer in spiritual direction as a way of expressing feelings without being willing or able to own or explore them and, if the sessions are to be genuinely fruitful, then this could perhaps be the subject of discussion—or challenge—by the director.

As in the case of prayer in therapy, there are also questions of power in the relationship between director and directee and I would therefore suggest the wisdom of considerable reflection about whose agenda is being served when praying in the spiritual direction context. Praying with another person is an extremely intimate act and, as with all intimate acts, there is the danger of, and potential for, an element of abuse to be present.

However, whether or not explicit prayer is to form part of the direction process, it is my practice during our initial discussion to advise all new directees that I will be including them in my personal prayers between sessions.

Prayer and spiritual practice for the therapist/spiritual director

Having considered the question of praying with, for, and about our clients and directees, I should also like to raise questions about the possibility of our clients and directees praying for us, either overtly or covertly. I know of several occasions when this has been the case: for example, a spiritual directee heard from another source that I had experienced a bereavement and sent me a card expressing sympathy and prayer; in another case, a client said he would be offering prayer for me when I was taking a holiday. I have been touched on these occasions, which I have seen as examples of the real "me" meeting the real "her/him" in Clarkson's person-to-person modality of the therapeutic relationship and as evidence of the mutuality of our co-creation.

Worthington, writing in Sperry (2001, p. 186) explores the question of how therapists cope with their work unless they have something they can call on that is somehow greater than themselves, that is, something that we might know as God. Both West (2004) and Thorne (2002) stress the importance of some form of personal spiritual discipline for therapists in order to work at spiritual depth with clients. Whether we see "God" as an external interventionist Being or as an internalised concept—as, in St Augustine's descriptive words, "more intimate with me than I am to myself" (2008, 3:6:11)—our relationship with whatever we choose to call the Divine is developed through our personal spiritual practice.

While the question of whether it is wise, ethical, and helpful to pray with or for clients and directees raises many different issues for consideration, and despite the fact that we sometimes seek binary "yes"/"no" answers, the imperative for Christian therapists and directors to have some personal prayer practice would seem pretty compelling. The necessity for adequate self-care is considered an ethical requirement and I would suggest that, for those who profess a specific faith and who are interested in bringing this faith to bear on their whole life—including their work—part of that self-support would inevitably include such spiritual practices as are fundamental to that faith. My own prayer life and spiritual practice thus become a core part of my self-support strategies and I am aware of a deficiency when I neglect them (which, regrettably, I often do).

Conclusion

The very idea of praying with a client is often seen as taboo and I suspect that there are few trainings in the United Kingdom where it would be considered an acceptable intervention—and I am not suggesting that this should necessarily change. However, this taboo may result in a climate where the practice of prayer will remain hidden and undisclosed and it is, perhaps, because of this aura of disapproval that many therapists do not feel comfortable taking the subject to supervision, thus compounding the whole sense of secrecy. Only when we can talk openly about the practice of prayer in a therapeutic context will we truly be able to evaluate the positive and negative outcomes that result. Perhaps this is an area where therapists have much to learn from spiritual directors.

Having said that, I would not dismiss the possibility of prayer in therapy and would agree with Gubi when he says: "What I have discovered is that prayer does have a place in ethical practice. What stops me from integrating prayer in my own practice is 'me'. To do so means that I have to question some cherished beliefs and assumptions that have been instilled in me from my training as a counsellor" (2008, p. 203).

Whether or not to pray with a therapy client or spiritual directee is a boundary issue and, as with all boundary issues, the interests of the client/directee are paramount. Therefore, whatever our personal views of this question may be, and whatever we might consider to be helpful, the decision about whether or not prayer is included in the session must ultimately rest with them. However, we have an ethical duty to pay attention to possible contraindications and to ensure that clients are properly informed about potential consequences. I do not consider it sufficient just to say that the client can decide without fully accepting my professional responsibilities. Perhaps Christian therapists need to reflect carefully on this subject while praying for clarity and wisdom about their own practice.

CHAPTER NINE

Training: or should it be formation?

"Untilled ground, however fertile, will bring forth thistles; so also the mind of man."

—St Teresa of Avila 1515–1582

Introduction

Whenever I see a chapter headed "Training", my immediate expectation is that I shall be reading a discussion of the pros and cons of different content material and that, by the end of the chapter, I will probably have some idea of what might be considered to be the "ideal" curriculum for a training programme. I'm afraid that, while I do have some ideas about what might usefully be included as part of the training experience, I am reluctant to prescribe specific topics, and the main focus of this chapter will be to emphasise the primacy of integrating spirituality into an holistic curriculum. This inevitably assumes that individual practitioners have engaged, at least to a certain extent, with their own personal integration, which therefore becomes the essential underpinning ingredient of any training programme. As McLeod, drawing on the work of Smail (1978) and Lomas (1981), states, "theory and techniques must be assimilated into the person of the therapist" (1998, p. 215).

I am therefore advocating that the idea of *formation* instead of *training* is more relevant and appropriate, implying as it does a process of development and growth, rather than merely the acquisition of knowledge and skills.

Overview of current training in psychotherapy and spiritual direction

There is very little hard evidence about how much spirituality is included in current psychotherapy and counselling training programmes. In fact, when, in 2011, a questionnaire was circulated by the Association of Pastoral and Spiritual Care and Counselling, researching the inclusion of spirituality in BACP accredited courses, the response was under 10% and the evidence given suggested that, in the main, spirituality was included in the context of addressing diversity issues (www.apscc.org.uk). Earlier, West stated: "A number of courses will briefly touch on spirituality and/or religion as an optional part of the course or deal with it in time set aside for cross-cultural issues. Either way it receives insufficient coverage which I think might well reflect limitations and biases amongst the trainers" (2004, p. 16).

I am not aware of any research into the content of spiritual direction training programmes in the United Kingdom. It would seem that the number of contact hours varies enormously, as do other course requirements, as well as expectations about giving and receiving spiritual direction. In some cases I have had difficulty in obtaining information about the content of courses. If courses are charging relatively large amounts of money, then potential students have a right to know what they are signing up for and this is another example of the fact that what is being offered in the Christian world is less than would be considered acceptable in a secular setting.

Psychotherapy training

Writing in a United States context, Pargament (2007, pp. 190–192) suggests that, in order for psychotherapists to practise spiritually integrated therapy, four elements are necessary: knowledge, openness and tolerance, self-awareness, and authenticity. It is interesting to note that three of the four are more about personal qualities than about theoretical knowledge. He later points out that courage is also necessary if we are genuinely to engage with spiritual practices and traditions that are unfamiliar and different from our own (ibid., p. 335). Swinton calls for those engaged in working with mental health issues to be bilingual, fluent in psychological language, and also in "the language of spirituality that focuses on issues of meaning, hope, value, connectedness and transcendence" (2001, p. 174). Again the suggestion is that the requirements for good practice relate to affective qualities rather than theoretical knowledge.

As a supervisor, I have noticed that practitioners– experienced *and* trainees—can usually describe how they work with issues of race, culture, sexual orientation, and disability—but relatively few of them can express themselves nearly as clearly on questions of spirituality. This may indicate that they have not reflected sufficiently on their own attitudes and personal experience in this area, suggesting that it is not seen as particularly relevant to the work of psychotherapy. I am curious to know whether this is because of historical attitudes influencing the culture of training establishments or, alternatively, because of the views of individual trainers and course directors—or a combination of both. Whatever the underlying cause, I would challenge all those involved in psychotherapy education to review both their personal and professional practice in relation to this aspect of human experience in order to adopt a more holistic approach.

As has been discussed in Chapter Three, there is encouraging evidence that attitudes amongst mental health workers towards spirituality are beginning to change and I am sure that this is reflected in some training programmes. However, I have no doubt that there are still some courses where the subject of spirituality in general, and religion in particular, is still at best marginalised and at worst either ignored or pathologized.

Having said that, I am not advocating that the curriculum should include a course in comparative religion. While it would seem both impossible and undesirable to attempt to train therapists to be expert in details of different faiths and religious practice, it seems reasonable that they are able to approach the subject of spirituality with confidence and competence. In order to do so, therapists need to have sufficient knowledge and information (and curiosity) to enquire how spirituality is manifested in the life of their clients, and to do this sensitively and intelligently necessitates insight into their own personal spiritual experience. As well as enhancing the psychotherapeutic process, this will also help therapists to evaluate whether they are the appropriate person to work with a particular client—or, indeed, whether therapy is an appropriate intervention at all, or whether a referral to a faith professional might be more helpful.

Spirituality and the therapist's personal development

In order to develop competence in the area of spirituality, I would also advocate that trainees should be expected to explore their own spiritual journey and encouraged to engage with some form of spiritual practice as part of their personal development. They might, for example, undertake a mindfulness programme as suggested by Kabat-Zinn (1990) or join a number of faith communities to experience a variety of spiritual practices. It might be worth therapists reflecting on the fact that the idea of going to a psychotherapist is just about as alien to some as the idea of going to church, synagogue, or mosque might seem to them; taking steps to engage with such a new experience might be very enlightening.

This deliberate attempt to gain understanding of what is often so central to the values, philosophy, and worldview of many clients would be a big challenge for many therapists. However, once the relationship can encompass the spiritual dimension, then the therapeutic skills of the competent practitioner will come into play in a way that will be no different from those in evidence when dealing with any other material. However, if the therapist cannot authentically get beyond holding negative feelings towards spiritual or religious material, then it would seem unlikely that the therapy will have a positive outcome. But would a similar view towards race, gender, or sexual orientation be permitted in a therapist? The answer is "no" and I would therefore question whether anyone holding critical views about spirituality should actually be practising at all—this does not mean to say that everyone has to share the same views, but that, as in other areas of life, a non-judgmental approach to a client's choices and views must be accepted and honoured.

Pargament suggests that therapists should be encouraged to prepare their own spiritual autobiography and provides the following questions as guidelines:

- What are my deepest values and what do I strive for in my life?
- What do I hold sacred?
- How did I discover the sacred?
- How has my larger family and institutional religious context shaped my attitude toward spirituality and religion?
- How have I tried to develop and sustain myself spiritually over the years?
- What kinds of struggles have I encountered in the process of developing and conserving my spirituality?
- What kinds of spiritual transformations have I experienced, if any?
- Where do I currently stand in the search for the sacred?
- What are the areas of spiritual integration and disintegration in my life?
- In what ways has my spirituality affected my life? In what ways has it not affected my life?
- What are my areas of spiritual strength and vulnerability in working with clients?
- Are there clients from particular spiritual or religious backgrounds whom I may not be able to help? (2007, p. 336).

Similarly West states unequivocally that "part of the training therapists need is to explore their countertransference responses to spirituality and religion" (2000, p. 17), and Richards & Bergin (1997, p. 338) demand a minimum level of training, including both religious issues and diversity and a requirement of supervision with supervisors with expertise in this area. This does not seem to be an unreasonable expectation for United Kingdom training programmes.

My plea, therefore, is for a change of heart, an increase in openness, tolerance and authenticity, together with the development of personal self-awareness on the part of therapists and trainers.

As previously indicated, it is obviously not possible for any one therapist to become an expert in all details of different faiths and religious practice and, indeed, there can be dangers in including such specific subjects in the curriculum of training courses, leading to assumptions about knowledge and understanding that could be quite erroneous and misleading. Even within a particular faith community, there can be many nuances and interpretations of doctrine and practice and the important thing is for therapists to approach these matters with an open mind and to be curious to learn *from their clients* what their personal understanding and interpretation might be and what impact this is having on their life.

Towards competence and confidence

However, in order that psychotherapists can develop appropriate confidence and competence in this area, there are some subjects which could usefully be the focus of specific training, in order to provide sufficient underpinning knowledge and a sound theoretical basis for integrating spirituality into psychotherapy. In a list of such topics I would include introductions to the following:

- Faith development, with particular emphasis on the work of Fowler/ Jamieson.
- The psychology of religion.
- How to take a spiritual history.
- Power in the therapeutic relationship.
- An introduction to the principles and practice of spiritual direction.

I would also suggest that signposting trainees to available resources on the subject of spirituality should be included, as with any other topic on the curriculum. These resources might include The Royal College of Psychiatry Special Interest Group website; Spirituality Matters website; BACP Information Sheet G13 Working with Issues of Faith, Religion and Spirituality.

Faith development

Both Fowler (1995) and Jamieson (2004) offer models and frameworks which provide theoretical knowledge and understanding of the experience that some clients face when wrestling with spiritual issues.

Fowler's *Stages of Faith* (1995), in which the author maps faith development against Erikson's model of human development, makes a particularly important contribution to the literature and to our understanding of spiritual integration. While his writing can perhaps be criticized for taking rather a linear approach, it provides an excellent foundation for theoretical thinking on this subject.

Jamieson also explores the process of faith development but with a particular emphasis on the experience of those who, for a variety of reasons, "outgrow" or become disenchanted with those elements of formalised religion which have previously given meaning to their lives and supported them spiritually. This is an experience that can be very destabilising, providing the catalyst that propels people into therapy and is, therefore, of particular relevance and importance to therapists.

The psychology of religion

It is perhaps difficult to know exactly what should be included in an attempt at an introductory overview to the psychology of religion. However, the work of Allport & Ross (1967), Bryant (1983), James (1961), and Johnston (1974), and, more recently, Corbett, (1996), Pargament (2007), Richards & Bergin (1997), and West (2000 & 2004), provide underpinning knowledge, together with Nelson's impressive publication (2009), which gives a comprehensive overview of the subject.

How to take a spiritual history

Probably the most practical contribution to helping therapists develop their confidence and competence in integrating spirituality into their practice lies in the area of taking a spiritual history. Once spirituality is seen as an accepted (and acceptable) element of therapy, then clients will refer to it or not, depending on their personal experience. It would therefore seem essential that they are "given permission" to bring their spiritual lives into the therapy room from the outset. Taking a spiritual history as part of the initial consultation offers clients such permission and it therefore seems vital that therapists develop some sort of framework for enquiry. While the following models may all need to be modified according to individual circumstances, they do include ideas and interventions that can usefully be adopted.

Culliford (2007, p. 214) and Culliford and Eagger (in Cook, Powell & Sims, 2009, p. 16ff) draw our attention to a number of models of taking a spiritual history, pointing out that it is the style of these that varies rather than the actual content and that they act more as aides-memoire than exact prescriptions. For those therapists whose practice would include taking a detailed initial history and who wish to include a spiritual element, they draw attention to the fact that quantitative data is not in itself sufficient; in order to be made meaningful it needs to be "interpreted, organised, integrated with theory" (ibid., p. 20). The first three items on the following list have been developed in a United Kingdom context while the subsequent two models have their origins in north America:

1. The Royal College of Psychiatrists' leaflet (2010) (www.rcpsych.ac.uk/ mentalhealthinformation/therapies/spiritualityandmentalhealth. aspx).
2. *A Guide to the Assessment of Spiritual Concerns in Mental Healthcare.* Eagger (2005, revised 2009).
3. *FAITH mnemonic: spiritual history-taking made easy.* Neely, N. and Minford, E. (2009, pp. 181–185).
4. *HOPE mnemonic: a Practical Tool for Spiritual Assessment.* Anandarajah, G. and Hight, E. (2001, pp. 7–11).
5. *FICA—Taking a Spiritual History.* Puchalski, C. and Romer, A. (2000).

Drawing on the work of those listed above, my own list of questions that might usefully be explored, either explicitly or implicitly, during the initial meeting with a client is as follows:

• What is the client's metaphysical world view?
• What values and beliefs help the client in living life to the full?
• Does the client hold any explicit spiritual/religious views?
• What would the client like to tell me about their spiritual/religious beliefs?
• What, if any, is the client's experience of religious practice both in childhood and later?
• Does the client have a current religious affiliation or practice?

Power in the therapeutic relationship

The question of the power structures that underpin the social culture of the United Kingdom is addressed in Chapter Seven. How power in the therapeutic relationship is understood within different models of therapy and how this may be experienced by clients, is also discussed.

An introduction to the principles and practice of spiritual direction

I am mindful of the demands on time in any training course. However, in order to equip therapists to engage with their clients' spirituality, basic information about the following would be helpful:

- Awareness that spiritual direction exists and how to access it.
- Understanding of the purpose and process of spiritual direction.
- Recognition of different models of spiritual direction (e.g., Ignatian, Benedictine etc).
- Resources to help therapists develop their knowledge of the subject as appropriate (e.g., websites of The Retreat Association, the London Centre for Spirituality, Spiritual Directors International, Soulfriend).

Training in spiritual direction

In order to integrate spirituality into psychotherapy training, the main requirement is a shift in attitude rather than the introduction of substantial amounts of theoretical material into the curriculum; this is not quite the same in the case of spiritual direction. However, a change in thinking is just as necessary if there is to be a more robust approach to the inclusion of psychological issues in both the primary and on-going training of spiritual directors. As Jones says: "it would be a poor spiritual director who did not have at least an intuitive knowledge of his psychological self and was unable to use some of the insights of psychotherapy in spiritual direction" (1982, p. 41). I would suggest that there is now an even stronger case for the importance of an underpinning of psychological knowledge.

I would see the shift in attitude focusing on the very basic question of whether or not one can be *trained* to be a spiritual director, which is still the subject of debate in some circles, reflecting the view of Kenneth Leech (1977) when he considered that the need for training in spiritual direction was very limited, a view shared by Ball (1996, Chapter Eight), who seems critical of formalised training programmes.

It is not uncommon for clergy to consider that their training for priesthood also prepares them to offer spiritual direction—a view which perhaps demonstrates a basic misunderstanding of the purpose and process of spiritual direction. The experience of spiritual direction can be a potent one, leading to profound changes in an individual's life, and to be accompanying a directee in this process involves responsibilities for competent practice that should not be underestimated. The provision of adequate training therefore seems to be imperative. As St Teresa of Avila states: "Although learning may not seem necessary in a director, my opinion has always been, and always will be that every Christian should endeavour to consult some learned person ... and the greater his learning the better. Those who take the path of prayer have great need of learning; and the more spiritual they are, the greater the need" (1957, p. 95).

Thornton would seem to share St Theresa's view on the primacy of knowledge when he says: "Knowledge comes before anything, including personal holiness ..." However, I do not share his somewhat idiosyncratic view towards training with its emphasis on the necessity for moral theology and the primacy of "progression" (1984, p. 94). However, King (2011, p. 20) is of the opinion that, while training can enhance a natural gift for spiritual direction, a director cannot be created by training alone, and I would agree that theoretical knowledge alone will not result in a creative and effective practitioner.

The whole idea of training in spiritual direction is a relatively new one and courses vary enormously in requirements, length, content, and quality. In the absence of any national organising or accrediting body for spiritual direction, it is difficult to gain an accurate overall picture of training courses being offered across the United Kingdom. However, anecdotal evidence—and the fact that the total number of training hours and course requirements of even the longest training programmes is nowhere near that of a psychotherapy training—suggests that, while basic listening skills are included as part of trainings, there is relatively little in-depth input on psychological process and theory in most spiritual direction courses. However, it is also worth noting that spiritual direction training programmes will usually include a number of trained therapists, certainly more than the number of spiritual directors undertaking therapy training.

As has already been discussed in Chapter Six, I would suggest that there are areas of knowledge and expertise that need to be included in all spiritual direction trainings in the interests of developing competent and safe ethical practice. These would include:

- Indicators of common mental health problems that might suggest the necessity for referral.
- Sufficient psychological knowledge to undertake a competent risk assessment with particular reference to indicators of depression.

- Knowledge and understanding of unconscious process (transference, countertransference, projection, projective identification, parataxic distortion, defences).
- Knowledge and understanding of the psychological significance of certain experiences that frequently become the focus of spiritual direction (e.g., sexuality, bereavement, anger, shame, etc.).
- Power in the spiritual direction relationship.
- Understanding of principles underpinning ethical practice and decision making.
- Knowledge of legal requirements that might be relevant to the practice of spiritual direction.

These are all issues that have already been discussed in this book and which, in the interests of safe, ethical and legal practice, cannot be ignored by those offering spiritual direction training programmes. However, I can already hear howls of dismay from some spiritual directors, unwilling even to reflect on the possible dangers inherent in incompetent practice, but I nevertheless maintain my stance that, if it is considered necessary for psychotherapists to have an in-depth understanding of unconscious processes, then it seems unsatisfactory for spiritual directors to be any less well equipped by their training.

While courses may, rightly, pay considerable attention to the theory and traditions, as well as skills and techniques, of spiritual direction, there may be an assumption that the students' personal spiritual growth is being attended to elsewhere. Most courses have an expectation that students will have their own spiritual director but, in the absence of any structure for national recognition, it is impossible to know what the directee's experience will be and to what degree their needs will be met.

Supervision

The contribution that supervision can make to training and professional development should not be underestimated. In supervision, therapists can gain considerable knowledge and insight into the whole area of spirituality and, similarly, spiritual directors can develop their understanding of psychological matters. However, this obviously depends on the attitudes and expertise of the supervisor so it is also worth considering how supervision trainings may need to be developed to include the subject of spirituality.

This is despite the fact that, in the case of spiritual direction in the UK, recognition of the importance and relevance of supervision is still in its infancy and supervision training is somewhat hard to find. It is to be hoped that supervision gives an opportunity for therapists and directors to explore issues arising from their practice in a safe space and to examine their own attitudes and responses to such issues. However, West (2000, p. 11) suggests that high quality supervision of spiritual issues may be thin on the ground and, as we have seen, it is a subject that is inadequately addressed in training courses. So, while supervision has the potential to offer important help and support, it may in itself present its own unique difficulties because supervisors may be neither well informed nor sympathetic to this type of material.

In the case of those therapists—both trainees and qualified—who work in settings where a supervisor is allocated, they may find themselves limited in what they can present in supervision for fear that they will be severely criticised. One supervisee with whom I worked had struggled for a year with a supervisor prescribed by her employer who considered any reference to spirituality to be a defence and evidence of negative thought processes which needed to be changed. Perhaps the potential difficulties inherent in finding suitable supervision are summed up by West: "In terms of psychospiritual work this will be impossible and possibly destructive if the supervisor is not respectful of religion and spirituality or welcoming of the broad sweep of the supervisee work in that domain" (2004, p. 148). West suggests six possible ways of dealing with problems associated with the supervision of spiritual material:

1. Play down the spiritual element of the client's material (with the inevitable risks to the client that this entails as well as the undermining of the supervisory relationship).
2. Have two supervisors, one to supervise the therapy and a second to supervise the spiritual element—an unworkable solution with inherent splitting.
3. Limit therapy to the non-spiritual element of the work and take the spiritual part elsewhere which, West suggests, feels unethical in that the client would be denied what we know would be helpful.
4. Find a supervisor with experience of working with spiritual issues.

5. Engage in training in a specifically spiritual model of therapy which would also offer its own framework of supervision.
6. Accept that there are no easy answers to the above dilemmas. (2000, p. 129).

Supervision is an accepted part of psychotherapeutic practice; the same cannot be said for spiritual direction. While, to their credit, many directors do make arrangements for group or individual supervision, this is not universally the case and the importance of on-going professional development and learning in this context is not generally appreciated. As we have already seen, there may be several factors that contribute to the prevailing view that supervision of spiritual direction is unnecessary:

- Lack of knowledge about psychological influences.
- Reluctance to acknowledge the importance of psychological influences.
- Reluctance towards anything that speaks of "professionalism".
- Reluctance towards charging, thus limiting the possibilities of rigorous professional development.

In this connection, Ruffing draws our attention to the value of supervision: "Because of the nature of spiritual direction, supervision is not merely a psychological process, but a spiritual one as well. Directors are profoundly affected by directees" (2000, p. 169), and the whole subject of the supervision of spiritual direction is addressed very helpfully in Conroy's (1995) book, *Looking into the Well: Supervision of Spiritual Directors*, and also in Bumpus and Langer (Eds.) (2005), *Supervision of Spiritual Directors*.

In addition to regular supervision, perhaps one of the best ways to support ourselves is through our own spiritual direction or therapy. When spiritual directors acknowledge the importance of unconscious psychological processes, it will also be important for them to have the opportunity to examine and explore these aspects of their work in supervision. It therefore follows that they may need to seek out supervisors who have the knowledge and expertise to address this element of direction. The fact that supervision is not seen as essential, or even desirable, together with the limited opportunities for the training of supervisors of spiritual direction, would seem to indicate that there is a long way to go in this area.

Conclusion

More research into the integration of spirituality into psychotherapy training, as well as into the inclusion of psychological issues into spiritual direction courses, is clearly needed. With so little reliable evidence, it is impossible to have a full and accurate picture of the current situation in the United Kingdom, as much of the information that is available is anecdotal and unverified. I fear that such research may be a long time coming because of the reluctance of some course providers and trainers to provide disclosure, together with an historical attitude of suspicion towards the subject.

Similarly, research relating to spiritual direction training programmes would be very valuable so that a picture of what is currently on offer could be seen, and realistic and meaningful comparisons between what providers are actually offering could be made. I suspect that any reluctance to engage with research may be because of the resistance to accountability that has previously been described.

CHAPTER TEN

My heretical question: can spiritual direction be considered a modality of psychotherapy?

"*Everybody has won and all must have prizes.*"

—Dodo Bird in *Alice in Wonderland*

Similar or different?

Despite the fact that there is currently an energetic movement in the United Kingdom to encourage the inclusion of spirituality in mental health care and therapy (see Chapters One and Three), there still seems to be a culture in which the differences between spiritual direction and therapy are considered to outweigh the similarities. For example, Moon and Benner (2004) invited representatives of a number of church denominations to identify what differentiates the practice of spiritual direction, psychotherapy, and pastoral counselling in terms of presenting problem, goals, procedure, and resources. While I recognise that the context of this work is north American, I find some of the distinguishing features offered almost unrecognisable in my own professional practice, particularly the assumption that there is little potential for spiritual growth in therapy. I have therefore come to the following conclusions:

That, while the content material brought by clients and directees to psychotherapy and spiritual direction may differ, the process is more similar than different.

The differences between the two disciplines lie mainly in questions of boundaries, contracts, and the current lack of agreed standards of ethical and competent practice in the field of spiritual direction.

That some psychotherapists are reluctant to address, or even acknowledge, issues of spirituality with their clients.

That each of the two enterprises has much to offer the other.

If, as I believe, it is the relationship between therapist and client, director and directee,—and the process that takes place within this relationship—that is the significant factor in therapy and spiritual direction, then the differences between the two activities can be seen to be less important and relevant. Much that has been written about this relationship can be summarised in the word "love"—a particular form of love I grant you, but a love that puts the other first with a desire for their well-being, and offering care and attention. Clinical psychologist Smail goes so far as to say that "The way to alleviate and mitigate distress is for us to *take care of* the world and the other people in it, not to *treat* them" (1998, p. 1, original italics). Johnston says that "the principal element in healing is not the psychological process … What is therapeutic is the experience of loving and being loved" (1974, p. 121). Jones writes of the apprenticeship which "involves both an intellectual as well as an emotional involvement in the art of loving" (1982, pp. 77–78).

Therapists take for granted the fact that their clients will present with a variety of seemingly different problems, yet they are happy to work across a range of issues, for example, relationship, addiction, loss, anger management, depression, etc., and I would suggest that, while the content and language may be different, the process and relationship are similar. As Foster says, "Spiritual direction is concerned with the whole person and the interrelationship of all life" (1989, p. 232), and I doubt that many psychotherapists would disagree that this could just as easily be said of their practice. My suggestion would therefore be that perhaps a more appropriate word to describe any perceived divergence between psychotherapy and spiritual direction would be "distinctive" rather than "different".

Nevertheless, I am aware that many psychotherapists and spiritual directors would not share my view, insisting that the differences outweigh the similarities, but I have noticed that they are often those who have not personally engaged with both experiences, some having had therapy and others having had spiritual direction but not usually both. When I talk with people who have engaged significantly with both, the view that they are more similar than different is borne out. This is also the conclusion reached by Gubi (2010):

> The data ... demonstrate that Counselling and Spiritual Accompaniment are similar in the quality of encounter, have some distinctiveness depending on the agenda, and that Spiritual Accompaniment has some deficits that need to be addressed in order to offer ethical and theologically-competent practice. (2010, p. 54)

My own experience of both giving and receiving spiritual direction and psychotherapy leads me to agree with this statement and I hope that I have been able to offer evidence to support this view in the preceding chapters. Others agree, for example, Jones who writes that "As a spiritual director, I know I need the expertise, the diagnostic skill of the psychotherapist; the psychotherapist also needs something that the spiritual director has to offer: the dimension of worship, adoration, and mystery in the face of the Other who is God, and of the other who is his fellow human being"(1982, p. 54).

And he also says:

> I tried to write a paper to show a clear and unequivocal demarcation line between therapy and spiritual direction. ... I failed miserably in my task to separate the psychological from the spiritual. Instead, I began to realize the enormous area of overlap between therapy and spiritual direction in the common concern for integrity, harmony, and radiance. (ibid., pp. 32–33)

Hart would also seem to agree:

> In sum, when psychotherapy and spirituality are both sound, they are united in their goal of promoting human well-being. They are not separate realms, and they are certainly not opposed. The best way to think of their relationship is to envision spirituality as the wider frame of meaning, value, and power within which psychotherapy operates. (2002, p. 22)

Hart also comments that he shares Viktor Frankl's view that religion subsumes and encompasses psychotherapy (ibid., p. 26), and gives an example of when he considers he has been offering both therapy and spiritual direction: "For me, the healing purpose and the faith vision coalesce, so that I see myself as *always* doing both therapy and spiritual direction" (ibid., p. 119, italics mine).

However, having said that, I am suggesting that they are similar, not identical, just as different types of therapy may be. In the case of spiritual direction, the main differences would seem to emerge from an underlying reluctance to accept a greater level of accountability, which, as we have already seen, is labelled (with negative connotations) as "professionalization". As we have seen in the previous chapter, both Leech (1977) and Ball (1996) express views that are averse to formalised training and they both take a hostile stance towards spiritual direction becoming more professional.

It is, perhaps, very understandable that, when challenged to move into new territory, we may become defensive and cautious, clinging to old ways. My observation is that such reluctance often comes from clergy and the more traditional practitioners among the world of spiritual directors, and I find myself wondering whether this is a manifestation of a personal decline in confidence, probably unconscious, among church leaders, as adherence and loyalty to mainstream faith communities diminish. In a post-modern world where there seem to be few absolutes, individuals are less willing to accept unquestioningly the authority of others, leaving many clergy, brought up to expect a certain degree of respectful attention, feeling threatened and deskilled.

In my dealings with many spiritual directors, I have noticed a particular reluctance, even hostility, to any idea of competence-based registration and, while not setting out to advocate any particular framework for such registration, I am hoping that this book may play some small part in opening a conversation about such a possibility. Perhaps this is one place where the experience of the therapy world may have something to offer. However, I am also mindful of the fact that not all therapists consider registration to be altogether beneficial, either for themselves or for their clients.

Again, the difference some psychotherapists perceive between their work and that of spiritual directors would seem to centre on a reluctance towards addressing the spirituality of their clients and thus, inevitably, to aspects of material brought into the therapy room. It can also be seen that sometimes—although not always—the factors and events that may precipitate a client into seeking therapy may be different from those that nudge directees towards a spiritual director. However, these differences may not, in fact, be as evident as they first seem, and it is worth remembering Jung's statement, quoted in Chapter Three, that, bidden or unbidden, God is present.

As we have seen, some therapists and directors are unhappy, and sometimes unwilling, to see anyone who is also actively involved in the other activity, which puts the client/directee in the position of having to make a choice, possibly at a time when they are feeling particularly distressed and confused. This situation also seems to reinforce the split between therapy and direction and it could be argued that, if therapists were more spiritually informed, they would be able to contemplate working alongside a spiritual director in the overall interests of the client. Likewise, if directors were more psychologically educated they would have greater insight into the benefits of the integration of the spiritual aspects with the emotional and intellectual dimensions. I suppose ideally I would hope that many more spiritual directors will train as therapists and vice versa so that total integration will be the result, but I suspect we are a long way from that being the case.

I am therefore left with what may be considered by some to be an heretical question about whether spiritual direction might be considered to be a particular and specific modality of psychotherapy, with its own unique qualities and specialist practitioners, just as there are currently therapists who work exclusively with children, or with particular issues such as addiction, bereavement, or adoption. I put this question forward somewhat tentatively, but, nevertheless, it is one that I think should be given serious consideration, not least because of the implications that such an idea would have for both practices.

My heretical question: is spiritual direction a modality of therapy?

Many clients come into psychotherapy with personal development in mind rather than at a time of distress or psychological upheaval. Similarly, while many directees start to engage with spiritual direction with the expressed purpose of deepening their spiritual life and relationship with God, there are also many for whom the catalyst is emotional turmoil or a life crisis. So, in both contexts there may be motives of both problem solving and healing—or perhaps desire for increased self-awareness and for change.

While, as we have already seen, there are spiritual directors who are extremely suspicious of anything that suggests that they should take a more "professional" approach to their work and, at the same time, there are psychotherapists who are reluctant to embrace questions of spirituality in their work, there are also psychotherapists (and I would include myself in this group) who see therapy as an essentially spiritual activity during which the spiritual dimension of client and of therapist interact in a mysterious and even mystical way that is (unsurprisingly) beyond description (Gubi, 2008), (Thorne, 2002), (West, 2004). As West says: "What I find of interest is to view counselling and psychotherapy as spiritual practices" (2000, p. 51), which is also very much in line with Rogers' view that "I am compelled to believe that I, like many others, have underestimated the importance of this mystical, spiritual dimension" (1980, p. 130).

Common factors theory

Bearing the above in mind, I find myself drawing conclusions from Rosenzweig's (1936) work on common factors and outcomes in psychotherapy which led to what is known as "The Dodo bird verdict", and Luborsky et al.'s (1975) meta-analysis of different "schools", which led to the same conclusion, and the famous article "Comparative studies of psychotherapies: Is it true that 'everyone has won and all must have prizes'?" The conclusion reached was that the effectiveness of different therapies has to do more with common factors than with particular and specific practices.

Hubble, Duncan, and Miller (2002, p. *xvii*) identify their book, *The Heart and Soul of Change: What Works in Therapy*, as a handbook on the common factors necessary for effective therapy. Referring to the work of Frank (1973), they state:

> (he) placed therapy within the larger family of projects designed to bring about healing. He ... looked for threads joining such different activities as traditional psychotherapy, group and family therapies, inpatient treatment drug therapy, medicine, religiomagical healing in nonindustrialized societies, cults, and revivals (2002, p. 7).

the conclusion being that all forms of therapy should be considered as "a single entity".

Frank himself stated:

> The therapist's ability to help his patient depends partly on his self confidence, and this in turn depends on mastery of a particular conceptual scheme and its accompanying techniques. Since the leading theories of psychotherapy represent alternative rather than incompatible formulations, it is unlikely that any one of them is completely wrong. (1973, p. 342)

Frank & Frank suggest:

> Two such apparently different psychotherapies as psychoanalysis and systematic desensitization could be like penicillin and digitalis—totally different pharmacological agents suitable for totally different conditions. On the other hand, the active therapeutic ingredient of both could be the same analogous to two aspirin-containing compounds marketing under different names. We believe the second alternative is closer to the truth. (1991, p. 39)

They proposed that four conditions are necessary for an effective outcome in all the healing arts, both magical and scientific, namely:

1. An emotionally charged relationship with a helping person.
2. A setting judged to be therapeutic.
3. A rationale for the healing process.
4. Some form of ritual or process.

I would suggest that these four conditions are in evidence in spiritual direction and that spiritual direction represents yet another—compatible—formulation. I would therefore also argue that the imperative for practitioners to work towards "mastery of a particular conceptual scheme and its accompanying techniques" (Frank, 1973, p. 342) holds just as true for spiritual directors as for therapists. Achieving mastery (a demanding goal in any undertaking) requires dedication, hard work, and high-quality training and development.

As we have seen, at the heart of the practice of both spiritual direction and psychotherapy lies relationship—the relationship between directors and directees, therapists and clients. In the case of spiritual direction, most practitioners would also hold the belief that the central relationship is that between those involved and the Divine, the Other, God. So in both cases it is clear that there is an emotionally charged relationship.

Both psychotherapists and spiritual directors pay a great deal of attention to the setting in which they practice, with an intentional aim of creating a safe space in which the client/directee can feel free to talk in confidence. Consideration is also given to any images and objects in the room and the messages, either consciously or unconsciously, that may be picked up from these. This is just as relevant in the case of spiritual direction, meeting the second of Frank and Frank's four conditions.

When considering Frank and Frank's third condition, I would argue that the rationale in spiritual direction is more defined and mutually understood by director and directee than is often the case in therapy where the client may well not hold a great understanding but trusts that the therapist "knows what s/he's doing". Equally, while the ritual and the process in therapy are defined in terms of boundaries and time keeping—as well as by what is expected both of and by therapist and client during the session—the rituals involved in spiritual direction may be much more explicit, for example, prayers, lighted candles, icons, and other spiritual symbols.

Purpose, content, process, practitioners

Purpose

I should like to return to the assertion that the purpose of the two activities is very different, central to this difference being the fact that the focus of spiritual direction is the directee's relationship with God rather than any other factor. Nelson expresses this view very clearly:

> While both involve helping relationships marked by mutual trust and intimate disclosure, direction differs in its conceptualization of the nature of the helping relationship, as well as its goals and methods. Counselling is a ... dyadic relationship between counsellor and client ... Spiritual direction ... is a triadic relationship involving the director, the person in direction, and God. (2009, p. 479)

As already touched on in Chapter One, there are two points that I would want to make about this assertion; firstly, that psychotherapists acknowledge a multiplicity of relationships present in the therapy room, of which the relationship between client and therapist is the most obvious but by no means the only one. Both client and therapist bring many other significant relationships such as family, friends, work colleagues and employers, social contacts, and many more—and this list of relationships may well include their relationship with God.

Secondly, I would like to ask the question: "Is the difference between the purpose of therapy and that of spiritual direction any more different from the purpose between, for example, bereavement therapy and working with an eating disorder—or, for that matter, psychotherapy for personal development?" I do not think that a difference in purpose alone can be considered a distinction between spiritual direction and psychotherapy.

Content

If the purpose of psychotherapy and spiritual direction cannot be considered to be a defining distinction, then it follows that the content of the sessions is not sufficient to distinguish one from the other. And in any case, in my experience much of the material brought to spiritual direction is identical to that brought to psychotherapy and vice versa. In attending to their relationship with God, directees often focus on the day-to-day difficulties and challenges in exactly the same way that psychotherapy clients do and, similarly, the yearning to make meaning of life, which is so often central to psychotherapy, is described in exactly the same way in spiritual direction.

It is perhaps relevant to remind ourselves here of UKCP's statement that "Psychotherapy involves exploring feelings, *beliefs*, thoughts, and relevant events ..." (www.psychotherapyorg.uk) (italics mine). This statement clearly indicates that beliefs may be brought into therapy.

Process

If you asked two therapists, or two spiritual directors, for an explanation of what went on during their sessions you would get two different responses. I would suggest that the process of what occurs in, for example, a person-centred therapy session could be far more similar to a spiritual direction session than might be the case between what goes on in between a transpersonal therapist and a CBT therapist and their respective clients.

Practitioners

This raises an interesting question about whether it is essential for a spiritual director to have a personal Christian faith—or any faith at all. Ruffing lists the following qualities necessary in a spiritual director which would seem identical to those required in a therapist: "A high level of presence, empathy, unconditional love, challenge, respect" (2000, p. 172).

Again, at risk of being labelled a heretic, I would suggest that, as long as the director can be truly open to the spirituality and faith belief of the directee, then their personal belief systems do not need to match, and in any case it is quite possible for two people, both of whom identify themselves as Christians, to have very diverse views about what they believe and about the essence of their professed faith. It is also interesting to note Propst et al.'s (2002) research which shows better outcomes for CBT therapists who did not share their clients' religious views than for those who did.

My challenge to spiritual directors

My challenge to spiritual directors therefore is to acknowledge their potency while facing up to their fears about levels of competence and their resistance to practices and conventions that would make them more accountable to themselves, their directees, and to the wider community. This would involve a willingness to address all those questions about "professionalization" that have already been mentioned and to accept the necessity for longer and more psychologically aware training programmes. This would also involve giving consideration to the whole question of money and charging for spiritual direction: training costs money; supervision costs money; it therefore follows that achieving levels of competence costs money; and, while clergy may well be able to offer their services as spiritual directors free of charge, this is because they are already being paid a stipend which lay spiritual directors are not. This will involve decisions about charging directees, something which many directors are very reluctant to do—more, I suspect, because they themselves are uncomfortable talking about money than for any of the more altruistic reasons that they may offer to support their decision to work for nothing!

At a time when the subject of national registration of psychotherapy is on the agenda, the question of whether therapists should be defined by *title* or by *function* is being discussed. It may, therefore, be decided that *function* (that is, what goes on during the session) is the defining factor that identifies the therapeutic activity rather than *title* (that is, by what those engaged in this activity actually call themselves—psychotherapist, counsellor etc.). It could then follow that spiritual directors could fall into this category because of the process in which they engage with their directees. This would, inevitably, catapult spiritual directors into accepting greater accountability.

I would also like to suggest that raising standards of knowledge and practice to meet the needs of Christians in the twenty-first century need not deny or negate any of the strengths that are linked with the ancient tradition of spiritual direction. However, to stay locked in the historical past without being willing to appreciate wisdom and insights from other traditions does, perhaps, encourage a ghetto mentality. My proposition would be that, in learning from other traditions about good practice, spiritual directors will be in a better position to teach from their own wisdom and history. I would invite directors to identify the positive aspects that might emerge and to join in the conversation. I would also challenge the spiritual direction community to move towards adopting agreed standards for safe and ethical practice.

My challenge to psychotherapists

My challenge to psychotherapists is that they *challenge themselves to examine their attitudes* as individual practitioners to the whole question of spirituality in their clinical work; to take time to inform themselves about this subject and, as suggested in Chapter Nine, to pay attention to their own inner journey. This is something that needs to be explored from the inside out rather than addressed as a theoretical and abstract subject. I invite therapists to explore any antipathy they may have to this area, to identify the positive aspects that might emerge, and to join in the conversation in a respectful way that may help to avoid some of the negative aspects and pitfalls.

I would also challenge those for whom spirituality is very much part of their therapeutic work to find their voice and speak out about their experience and that of their clients. Reluctance to talk about this aspect of our work arises out of a fear of criticism, derision, or hostility that is not found in relation to any other subject that comes into the therapy room. I would also like therapists to have an expectation that their supervisors are willing and competent to address spirituality in supervision.

My invitation to both psychotherapists and spiritual directors

I would invite spiritual directors and psychotherapists to consider their attitudes to each other with a great deal of humility. These two practices are not in competition: they can be complementary if those involved are willing to become better informed about each others' particular strengths, gifts, and talents. One is not better than the other; both have something very valuable to offer and each can learn a great deal from the other.

So my invitation to both psychotherapists and spiritual directors is to co-operate and collaborate rather than compete. Would it be possible for therapists to do some form of "top up" training to become spiritual directors? Equally, could spiritual directors join parts of established therapy courses to enhance their training of psychological theory? I am sure that this is not impossible, but the first step must be for therapists and directors to be willing to take on such training—in fact actually to demand it (and, as we know, once there is a demand, the "market" will provide). This is a big challenge as it involves surrendering defended positions, examining attitudes that have been firmly held, and being open to change and willing to be changed.

In order for the above to happen, both therapists and directors need to lose their fears that their current practice may be seen as deficient and with room for development and improvement. Of course, our practice is always going to be less than perfect, but the more these issues are discussed openly, without defensiveness or apology and in a less fearful environment, then the more the understanding between both practices will develop and mutual learning take place.

Conclusion

What can we make of all the questions raised so far? For me, the primary focus must always be on those people who come to us for either therapy or spiritual direction. I am sure that spiritual directors and psychotherapists would be of one mind in stating that only the best we can offer will do. If we see our work in terms of vocation, then we will take this work very seriously, be fully committed, prepare, and study as much as we can.

As mentioned in the Preface, I hold a profound belief in the unique individuality of each person and I see both psychotherapy and spiritual direction as means through which this fundamental essence can be realised and developed. For me, this resonates with the words of St Francis de Sales: "Let us be what we are, and let us be it well, to do honour to the Master whose work we are" (1894, p. 359).

I am therefore left with two convictions that apply to both areas of my practice:

1. That my relationship with client or directee is central to our work together and it is in the safe and loving environment that both therapy and spiritual direction provide that healing can take place.
2. That clients and directees both deserve the best I can give them and it is therefore my duty to be as well trained, informed, and competent as I can be.

I am also left with questions about how the apparent suspicion that is evident in some practitioners might be dissolved and a deeper and more respectful understanding of the common factors between psychotherapy and spiritual direction may be developed. It is my hope that, if you have read to this point in the book, you will be willing to contribute to the continuing discussion and to increased collaboration between the two disciplines.

REFERENCES

Aelred of Riveaulx (1974). *Spiritual Friendship*. Kalamazoo, MI: Cistercian Publications.

Allport, G. W. & Ross, M. (1967). Personal religious orientation and prejudice. *Journal of Personality and Social Psychology, 5 (4)*: 432–443.

American Psychiatric Association (1994). *Diagnostic and Statistical Manual of Mental Disorders (DSM-IV-TR)* (4th edition text revised). Washington, DC: American Psychiatric Association.

Anandarajah, G. & Hight, E. (2001). Using the HOPE questions as a practical tool for spiritual assessment. *American Family Physician Jan 1. 63 (1)*: 81–89.

Anonymous (2001). *The Cloud of Unknowing and Other Works*. London: Penguin Classics.

Balint, M. (1968). *The Basic Fault*. London: Tavistock Publications.

Ball, P. (1996). *Journey into Truth*. New York: Mowbray.

Barry, W. A. (2004). *Spiritual Direction and the Encounter with God: A Theological Enquiry*. New York: Paulist Press.

Barry, W. A. & Connolly, W. J. (1984). *The Practice of Spiritual Direction*. New York: HarperCollins.

Benner, D. G. (2002). *Sacred Companions: The Gift of Spiritual Friendship and Direction*. Downers Grove, IL: InterVarsity Press.

139

Bergin, A. E. & Payne, I. R. (1991). Proposed agenda for a spiritual strategy in personality and psychotherapy. *Journal of Psychology and Christianity*, 10: 97–210.

Birmingham, M. & Connelly, W. J. (1994). *Witnessing to the Fire*. Kansas City: Sheed & Ward.

Bollas, C. (1987). *The Shadow of the Object: Psychoanalysis of the Unthought Known*. London: Free Association Books.

Bond, T. & Mitchels, B. (2008). *Confidentiality and Record Keeping in Counselling and Psychotherapy*. London: Sage.

Bond, T. & Sandhu, A. (2005). *Therapists in Court: Providing Evidence and Supporting Witnesses*. London: Sage.

British Association for Counselling and Psychotherapy (2010). *Ethical Framework for Good Practice in Counselling and Psychotherapy*. Lutterworth: BACP.

Bryant, C. (1983). *Jung and the Christian Way*. London: Darton, Longman & Todd.

Buber, M. (1958). *I and Thou*. Edinburgh: T & T Clark.

Bumpus, R. & Langer, R. B. (Eds.) (2005). *Supervision of Spiritual Directors: Engaging in Holy Mystery*. London: Morehouse Publishing.

Byrd, R. C. (1988). Positive therapeutic effects of intercessory prayer in coronary care unit population. *Southern Medical Journal 81* pp. 826–829.

Carroll, L. (1974). *Alice's Adventures in Wonderland & Through the Looking Glass*. London: Bodley Head.

Claridge, G. (2001). Spiritual experience: Healthy psychoticism? In: I. Clarke (Ed.), *Psychosis and Spirituality: Exploring the New Frontier* (pp. 90–106). London: Whurr.

Clarke, I. (Ed.). (2001). *Psychosis and Spirituality: Exploring the New Frontier*. London: Whurr.

Clarkson, P. (1995). *The Therapeutic Relationship*. London: Whurr.

Code of Conduct for Healthcare Chaplains in Northern Ireland (2011). http://www.dhsspsni.gov.uk/nihca-code_of-conduct.pdf [last accessed 26 January 2012].

Concise Oxford Dictionary (1964). Oxford: Oxford University Press.

Conroy, M. (1995). *Looking into the Well: Supervision for Spiritual Directors*. Chicago: Loyola University Press.

Cook, C., Powell, A. & Sims, A. (Eds.) (2009). *Spirituality and Psychiatry*. London: RCPsych. Publications.

Corbett, L. (1996). *The Religious Function of the Psyche*. Hove: Routledge.

Culliford, L. (2007). Taking a spiritual history. *Advances in Psychiatric Treatment*, 13: 212–219.

Culliford, L. & Eagger, S. (2009). Assessing spiritual needs. In: C. Cook, A. Powell. & A. Sims (Eds.), *Spirituality and Psychiatry* (pp. 16–38). London: RCPsych Publications.

Culligan, K. (2003). The dark night and depression. In: K. Egan (Ed.), *Carmelite Prayer: A Tradition for the Twenty-first Century* (pp. 119–138). Mahwah, NJ: Paulist Press.

cummings, e. e. (1991). In: Firmage, G. J. (Ed.), *Complete Poems* 1904–1962. New York: Liveright.

Dein, S. (2004). Working with patients with religious beliefs. *Advances in Psychiatric Treatment* 10: 287–255.

Dossey, L. (1993). *Healing Words: The Power of Prayer and the Practice of Medicine.* San Francisco, CA: HarperCollins.

Edwards, T. (2001). *Spiritual Director, Spiritual Companion.* Mahwah, NJ: Paulist Press.

Fleming, D. L. (1996). *The Spiritual Exercises: A Literal Translation and a Contemporary Reading.* Saint Louis, MO: The Institute of Jesuit Sources.

Foster, R. (1989). *Celebration of Discipline* (revised edition). London: Hodder and Stoughton.

Fowler, J. W. (1995). *Stages of Faith: The Psychology of Human Development and the Quest for Meaning.* San Francisco: Harper.

Frank, J. D. (1973). *Persuasion and Healing: A Comparative Study of Psychotherapy* (second edition). Baltimore: Johns Hopkins University Press.

Frank, J. D. & Frank, J. B. (1991). *Persuasion and Healing: A Comparative Study of Psychotherapy* (third edition). Baltimore: Johns Hopkins University Press.

Gordon, K. (2010). The route to becoming an adoption support agency. *The Psychotherapist, 44*: 4–5.

Green, T. H. (1979), *When the Well Runs Dry.* Notre Dame, IN: Ave Maria Press.

Griffith, J. L. & Griffith, M. E. (2002). *Encountering the Sacred in Psychotherapy: How to Talk with People about their Spiritual Lives.* New York: The Guilford Press.

Grof, C. & Grof, S. (Eds.) (1989). *Spiritual Emergency: When Personal Transformation becomes a Crisis.* Los Angeles: Tarcher.

Gubi, P. M. (2001). An exploration of the use of prayer in mainstream counselling. *British Journal of Guidance and Counselling, 29* (4): 425–434.

Gubi, P. M. (2002). Practice behind closed doors—challenging the taboo of prayer in mainstream counselling culture. *Journal of Critical Psychology, Counselling and Psychotherapy, 2* (2): 97–104.

Gubi, P. M. (2008). *Prayer in Counselling and Psychotherapy: Exploring a Hidden Meaningful Dimension.* London: Jessica Kingsley Publishers.

Gubi, P. M. (2010). A qualitative exploration of the similarities and differences between Counselling and Spiritual Accompaniment. [Unpublished dissertation]. Anglia Ruskin University.

Guntrip, H. (1957). *Psychotherapy and Religion.* New York: Harper and Brothers.

Harborne, L. (2006). Is the soul the last taboo? *The British Journal of Psychotherapy Integration: Re-claiming the Transpersonal in the Pyschotherapeutic Endeavour, 3* (1): 48–54.

Harborne, L. (2008). *Working with Issues of Spirituality, Faith or Religion.* BACP Information Sheet. Lutterworth: BACP.

Harris, W. S., Gowda, M., Kolb, J. W., Strychacz, C. P., Vacek, J. L., Jones, P. G., Forker, A., O'Keefe, J. H. & McCallister, B. D. (1999). A randomised, controlled trial of the effects of remote, intercessory prayer on outcomes in patients admitted to the coronary care unit. *Archives of Internal Medicine, 159:* 2273–2278.

Hart, T. (2002). *Hidden Spring: The Spiritual Dimension of Therapy.* Minneapolis, MN: Fortress Press.

Hawkins, P. & Shohet, R. (2006). *Supervision in the Helping Professions* (third edition). Maidenhead: Open University Press.

Hay, D. & Hunt, K. (2002). The spirituality of adults in Britain—Recent research. *Scottish Journal of Healthcare Chaplaincy, 5* (1): 4–9.

Herman, J. L. (1992). *Trauma and Recovery, from Domestic Abuse to Political Terror.* London: Pandora.

Holy Bible, (1973). *New International Version.* London: Hodder & Stoughton.

Hubble, M. A., Duncan, B. L. & Miller, S. D. (1999). *The Heart and Soul of Change: What Works in Therapy.* Washington, DC: American Psychological Association.

James, W. (1985). *The Varieties of Religious Experience.* London: Penguin Books.

Jamieson, A. (2004). *Journeying in Faith: In and Beyond the Tough Places.* London: SPCK.

Jamieson, A. (2007). *Chrysalis: The Hidden Transformation in the Journey of Faith.* Milton Keynes: Authentic Media.

Jenkins, C.A. (2011). When clients' spirituality is denied in counselling. In: W. West (Ed.), *Exploring Therapy, Spirituality and Healing.* Basingstoke: Palgrave MacMillan.

Johnston, W. (1974). *Silent Music.* Glasgow: William Collins.

Jones, A. (1982). *Exploring Spiritual Direction; an Essay on Christian Friendship.* San Francisco: Harper & Row.

Julian of Norwich (2003). *Revelations of Divine Love.* London: Penguin Classics.

Jung, C. G. (1933). *Modern Man in Search of a Soul* (Baines, C. Trans). London: Routledge & Kegan Paul.

Kabat-Zinn, J. (1990). *Full Catastrophe Living: How to Cope with Stress, Pain and Illness using Mindfulness Meditation.* London: Piatkus.

Kahn, M. (1997). *Between Therapist and Client: the New Relationship* (second edition). New York: St Martin's Press.

Kirschenbaum, H. & Henderson, V. (Eds.) (1990). *The Carl Rogers Reader.* London: Constable.

King, P. (2011). A gift for the church: The value of spiritual direction. *Mount Carmel: A Review of Spiritual Life Vol. 59 (1)*: 18–23.

Koenig, H. G. & Pritchett, J. (1998). Religion and psychotherapy. In: H. G. Koenig (Ed.), *Handbook of Religion and Mental Health.* California: Academic Press.

Kohut, H. (1971). *The Analysis of the Self.* New York: International Universities Press.

Lawrence, B. R. (2008). *The Brother Lawrence Collection: Practice and Presence of God, Spiritual Maxims, The Life of Brother Lawrence.* Radford, VA: Wilder Publications.

Lazarus, A. A. (1976). *Multimodal Behaviour Therapy.* New York: Springer.

Leech, K. (1977). *Soul Friend: A Study in Spirituality.* London: Sheldon Press.

Levinas (1983). *Of God Who Comes to Mind.* (Bergo, B., Trans). Palo Alto, CA: Stanford University Press.

Levison, C. Members of Steering Group. (2009). *Spiritual Care Matters.* Edinburgh, NHS Education for Scotland.

Lomas, P. (1981). *The Case for a Personal Psychotherapy.* Oxford: Oxford University Press.

Luborsky, L., Singer, B. & Luborsky, L. (1975). Comparative studies of psychotherapies: Is it true that "everyone has won and all must have prizes"? *Archives of General Psychiatry, 32*: 995–1008.

Lukoff, D. (1985). The diagnosis of mystical experiences with psychotic features. *Journal of Transpersonal Psychology, 17 (2)*: 155–181.

Magaletta, P. R. & Brawer, A. (1998). Prayer in psychotherapy: A model for its use, ethical considerations and guidelines for practice. *Journal of Psychology and Theology 26, 4*: 322–330.

Maroda, K. J. (2004). *The Power of Countertransference.* Hillsdale, NJ: The Analytic Press.

Masson, J. (1997). *Against Therapy.* London: Fontana.

Matthew, I. (1995). *The Impact of God: Soundings from St John of the Cross.* London: Hodder and Stoughton.

May, G. G. (1992). *Care of Mind, Care of Spirit*. (paperback edition) New York: HarperCollins.

May, G. G. (2005). *The Dark Night of the Soul*. (paperback edition) New York: HarperCollins.

McLeod, J. (1998). *An Introduction to Counselling* (second edition). Buckingham: Open University Press.

Mearns, D. & Cooper, M. (2005). *Working at Relational Depth in Counselling and Psychotherapy*. London: Sage.

Merton, T. (1960). *Spiritual Direction and Meditation*. Collegeville, MN: Liturgical Press.

Merton, T. (1961). *New Seeds of Contemplation*. New York: New Directions.

Mitchell, S. & Roberts, G. (2009). Psychosis. In: C. Cook, A. Powell & A. Sims (Eds.), *Spirituality and Psychiatry* (pp. 39–60). London: RCPsych. Publications.

Moon, G. W. & Benner, D. G. (Eds.) (2004). *Spiritual Direction and the Care of Souls*. Downers Grove, Il: InterVarsity Press.

Moore, T. (2004). *Dark Nights of the Soul: A Guide to Finding your Way through Life's Ordeals*. London: Piatkus Books Ltd.

Neely, D. & Minford, E. (2009). FAITH: spiritual history-taking made easy. *The Clinical Teacher 6*: 181–185.

Nelson, J. M. (2009). *Psychology, Religion, and Spirituality*. Valparaiso, IN: Springer.

O'Collins, G. (1995). *Second Journey* (third edition). Leominster, UK: Gracewing.

Palmer, M. (1997). *Freud and Jung on Religion*. London: Routledge.

Pargament, K. I. (2007). *Spiritually Integrated Psychotherapy: Understanding and Addressing the Sacred*. New York: Guilford Press.

Proctor, G. (2002). *The Dynamics of Power in Counselling and Psychotherapy: Ethics, Politics and Practice*. Ross-on-Wye, UK: PCCS Books.

Propst, L. R., Ostrom, R., Watkins., P, Dean, T. & Mashburn, D. (2002). Comparative efficacy of religious and nonreligious cognitive-behavioral therapy for the treatment of clinical depression in religious individuals. *Journal of Consulting and Clinical Psychology, 60*: 94–103.

Puchalski, C. & Romer, A. (2000). Taking a spiritual history allows clinicians to understand patients more fully. *Journal of Palliative Medicine, 3*: 129–137.

Richards, P. S. & Bergin, A. E. (1997). *A Spiritual Strategy for Counseling and Psychotherapy*. Washington, DC: American Psychological Association.

Roberts, L., Ahmed, I. & Hall, S. (2007). Intercessory prayer for the alleviation of ill health. *Cochrane Database of Systematic Reviews, Issue 1*, CD000368, doi: 10.1002/14651858. CD000368.pub2.

Roethke, T. (1975). *Collected Poems of Theodore Roethke.* New York: Anchor Books.

Rogers, C. R. (1951). *Client-Centred Therapy: Its Current Practice, Implications and Theory.* Boston, MA: Houghton Mifflin.

Rogers, C. R. (1978). *Carl Rogers on Personal Power: Inner Strength and Its Revolutionary Impact.* London: Constable.

Rogers, C. R. (1980). *A Way of Being.* Boston: Houghton Mifflin.

Rose, J. (2002). *Sharing Spaces? Prayer and the Counselling Relationship.* London: Darton, Longman & Todd.

Rosenzweig, S. (1936). Some implicit common factors in diverse methods in psychotherapy. *Journal of Orthopsychiatry, 6*: 412–415.

Rothschild, B. (2000). *The Body Remembers.* New York: W. W. Norton.

Rothschild, B. (2006). *Help for the Helper.* New York: W. W. Norton.

Ruffing, J. K. (2000). *Spiritual Direction: Beyond the Beginnings.* Mahwah, NJ: Paulist Press.

Saint Teresa (1957). *The Life of Saint Teresa.* (Cohen, J. M., Trans) Harmondsworth: Penguin Classics.

Schrock, D. (2009). *The Dark Night, Gift of God.* Scottdale, PA: Herald Press.

Sims, A. C. P. (1992). Symptoms and beliefs. *Journal of the Royal Society of Health 112(1)*: pp. 42–46.

Smail, D. (1978). *Psychotherapy: A Personal Approach.* London: Dent.

Smail, D. (1998). *Taking Care: An Alternative to Therapy.* London: Constable.

Smail, D. www.davidsmail.info/introfra.htm [last accessed 26 January, 2012].

Soulfriend, the Berkshire, Buckinghamshire and Oxfordshire Spiritual Direction Network website: www.soulfriend.org.uk [last accessed 31 January, 2012].

Sperry, L. (2001). *Spirituality in Clinical Practice—Incorporating the Spiritual Dimension in Psychotherapy and Counseling.* Philadelphia, PA: Brunner Routledge.

Spiritual Directors International: www.sdiworld.org [last accessed 31 January, 2012].

St Augustine (2008). *The Confessions of St Augustine.* Chadwick, H. (Ed). Oxford: Oxford Paperbacks.

St Francis de Sales (1894). *The Library of St Francis de Sales Volume 1 Letters to Persons in the World* (Mackey, H. B., Trans.) London: Burns & Oates.

Silver, A. W. (2003). *Trustworth Connections: Interpersonal Issues in Spiritual Direction.* Cambridge, MA: Cowley Publications.

Stern, D. (1985). *The Interpersonal World of the Infant: A View from Psychoanalysis and Developmental Psychology.* New York: Basic Books.

Styron, W. (1992). *Darkness Visible* London: Jonathan Cape.

Swinton, J. (2001). *Spirituality and Mental Health Care: Rediscovering a Forgotten Dimension*. London: Jessica Kingsley Publishers.

Tan, S. Y. (2004). Spiritual direction and psychotherapy: ethical issues. In: G. W. Moon. & D. G. Benner (Eds.), *Spiritual Direction and the Care of Souls* (pp. 187–204). Downers Grove, Il: InterVarsity Press.

The London Centre for Spirituality: www.spiritualitycentre.org [last accessed 31 January, 2012].

The Retreat Association: www.retreats.org.uk [last accessed 31 January, 2012].

Thorne, B. (2002). *The Mystical Path of Person-Centred Therapy: Hope Beyond Despair*. London: Whurr.

Thornton, M. (1984). *Spiritual Direction: a Practical Introduction*. London: SPCK.

UKCP www.psychotherapy.org.uk [last accessed 26 January 2012].

United Kingdom Council for Psychotherapy. (2006). *Code of Ethics.*

Van de Weyer, R. (1995). *The Dark Night of the Soul and The Living Flame of Love: St John of the Cross*. London: HarperCollins.

West, W. (2000). *Psychotherapy and Spirituality: Crossing the Line between Therapy and Religion*. London: Sage.

West, W. (2004). *Spiritual Issues in Therapy: Relating Experience to Practice*. Basingstoke: Palgrave Macmillan.

Wilson, G. B. (2008). *Clericalism, the Death of Priesthood*. Collegeville, MN: Liturgical Press.

Winnicott, D. W. (1975). *Through Paediatrics to Psycho-analysis*. New York: Basic Books.

INDEX